No AR

W9-DJQ-002

Social Issues
in Literature

The Abuse of Power
in George Orwell's
Nineteen Eighty-Four

Other Books in the Social Issues in Literature Series:

Social Issues
in Literature

The Abuse of Power
in George Orwell's
Nineteen Eighty-Four

Dedria Bryfonski, Book Editor

GREENHAVEN PRESS
A part of Gale, Cengage Learning

GALE
CENGAGE Learning™

Detroit • New York • San Francisco • New Haven, Conn • Waterville, Maine • London

Christine Nasso, *Publisher*
Elizabeth Des Chenes, *Managing Editor*

© 2010 Greenhaven Press, a part of Gale, Cengage Learning

Gale and Greenhaven Press are registered trademarks used herein under license.

For more information, contact:
Greenhaven Press
27500 Drake Rd.
Farmington Hills, MI 48331-3535
Or you can visit our Internet site at gale.cengage.com

For product information and technology assistance, contact us at

Gale Customer Support, 1-800-877-4253
For permission to use material from this text or product, submit all requests online at www.cengage.com/permissions

Further permissions questions can be emailed to permissionrequest@cengage.com

Articles in Greenhaven Press anthologies are often edited for length to meet page requirements. In addition, original titles of these works are changed to clearly present the main thesis and to explicitly indicate the author's opinion. Every effort is made to ensure that Greenhaven Press accurately reflects the original intent of the authors. Every effort has been made to trace the owners of copyrighted material.

Cover image by Allan Grant/Time & Life Pictures/Getty Images.

LIBRARY OF CONGRESS CATALOGING-IN-PUBLICATION DATA

The abuse of power in George Orwell's Nineteen eighty-four / Dedria Bryfonski, book editor.
    p. cm. -- (Social issues in literature)
    Includes bibliographical references and index.
    ISBN 978-0-7377-4805-5 (hardcover) -- ISBN 978-0-7377-4806-2 (pbk.)
    1. Orwell, George, 1903-1950. Nineteen eighty-four. 2. Power (Social sciences) in literature--Juvenile literature. 3. Totalitarianism and literature--Juvenile literature. 4. Dystopias in literature--Juvenile literature. I. Bryfonski, Dedria.
    PR6029.R8N49385 2010
    823'.912--dc22
                                                                    2009042503

Printed in the United States of America
2 3 4 5 6 7 14 13 12 11 10

Contents

Chapter 2: George Orwell's *Nineteen Eighty-Four* and the Abuse of Power

Chapter 3: Contemporary Perspectives on the Abuse of Power

Introduction

Published in 1948, just seven months before George Orwell died, *Nineteen Eighty-Four* is his best-selling and most influential work. In it, he brings the major themes and concerns he developed throughout his life into their most powerful, if bleakest, expression. Although Orwell places his novel in the future, the themes he develops are drawn from his past. George Orwell, the pseudonym of Eric Arthur Blair, had deeply held political beliefs and used his novels and essays as vehicles to express these beliefs. An understanding of certain formative life experiences aids in the appreciation of Orwell's political beliefs. It was through these experiences—involving totalitarianism, inhumanity, and propaganda—that he formed the views that would culminate in the publication of *Nineteen Eighty-Four*. In this work, he warns of the dangers of totalitarianism—not just in Soviet Russia, but in any country where a government assumes total control. The specific incidents in his life that critics cite as especially formative to Orwell are his years at a boarding school, serving as a policeman in Burma, living in poverty in Paris, fighting in the Spanish Civil War, and working as India editor for the British Broadcasting Corporation (BBC) during World War II.

From 1911 to 1916, Orwell was a scholarship student at St. Cyprian's, a preparatory boarding school. This was not a happy experience for the young Orwell, as he would later relate in the short story "Such, Such Were the Joys," a bitter account of boarding school life characterized by beatings, snobbery, favoritism, and arbitrary rules. Several critics have drawn parallels between the torture scenes in *Nineteen Eighty-Four* and the bullying that occurs at a British boarding school. His friend and biographer T.R. Fyvel asserts that Orwell supported this view. Fyvel states, "He was convinced that for people who had grown up among the safe conventions of democratic England—and the intelligentsia above all—the only English parallel for the nightmare of totalitarianism was the experience of a misfit boy in an English boarding school." The critic Richard J. Voorhees makes a further point. He finds "Such, Such Were the Joys" to be Orwell's protest against the tyranny, injustice, and cruelty he experienced at St. Cyprian's. These school experiences were responsible for developing in Orwell a hatred for inhumanity and the abuse of power. Voorhees calls "Such, Such Were the Joys," an attack on small-scale tyranny, while *Nineteen Eighty-Four* is an attack on large-scale tyranny.

Following his graduation from Eton College and with the encouragement of his family, Orwell became a police officer with the Indian Imperial Police in Burma. It proved to be an unfortunate choice of occupation for a sensitive young man, and he resigned his position after five years. His experiences in Burma, however, added to his development as a writer. Even before leaving the ship that transported him to India, Orwell was horrified to witness a "coolie" (a derogatory term for an Asian manual laborer) being kicked in the bottom by a white sergeant to the indifferent stares of white onlookers. He found it troubling to serve as a policeman enforcing British control of a native population and wrote about seeing "the dirty work of Empire at close quarters." He also found the responsibilities of a police officer, with the power of life or death over others, and the reality that people were often treated as inhuman objects, to be vastly troubling. British literary critic and editor of the *Times Literary Supplement* John Gross finds that "while the problem of dismantling the Empire remained one of his immediate political concerns, it is true that by the last years of his life it no longer deeply engaged his imagination as a creative writer. He was looking further ahead, and in *Nineteen Eighty-Four* he portrays a world in which an altogether more pervasive and more implacable form of imperialism has triumphed, with no prospect of its being overthrown."

On his return from Burma, Orwell made the decision to become a writer and moved to Paris where he wrote two novels that were never published and several short stories and essays and gathered the material for the Parisian section of the autobiographical work *Down and Out in Paris and London*. It was in Paris that Orwell had his only experience with real poverty. He was robbed of two hundred francs and for about ten weeks experienced hunger and desperation. Critic Richard Mayne states that "Paris had not only given him intense private experience; it had also, almost literally, plunged him into the concerns that made his career as a writer. Until then, he had been a potential latter-day [British writer John] Galsworthy, going on East-End 'expeditions' from a room in Notting Hill. Now, he had shared the life that he had looked at. In this sense, although he chose his pen-name three years later, Paris helped to make George Orwell out of Eric Blair."

Many critics cite the Spanish Civil War as a watershed event in the development of Orwell's political thinking. He went to Spain as a journalist to cover the war and ended up fighting as a member of the POUM (Workers Party of Marxist Unification) militia. He soon learned of a schism in the strategies of the left-wing coalitions fighting the fascists. Orwell believed the POUM was misrepresented by the Communists, but found it difficult to find an audience for his version of events. The periodical the *New Statesman*, for instance, refused to publish his coverage of the war, and his publisher rejected *Homage to Catalonia*, the book he wrote about his experiences in the war. His personal disillusionment with the Communist Party and the left-wing intelligentsia developed in Orwell a concern about the manipulation of history for political purposes. As British historian Sir Raymond Carr states, "Given this *suppressio veri* [suppression of the truth] by interested parties, how could true history be written? Propaganda would pass as truth; 'facts' could be manipulated. Those who monopolized communication could create their own history after the event—the nightmare of *Nineteen Eighty-Four*."

During World War II, Orwell served as India editor at the British Broadcasting Company, a job that he found frustrating, for he came to believe its purpose was to disseminate official propaganda rather than news. His friend William Empson, who also worked at the BBC, wrote, "The experience of being India editor continued to work on him, and the early parts of *Nineteen Eighty-Four* were evidently conceived as farce about it." The canteen at the Ministry of Truth is modeled after the BBC canteen. Some critics suggest that the fictional term "Big Brother" may be derived from the name of the Minister of Information, Brendan Bracken, who was known to subordinates as "B.B."

In an obituary that appeared in the *Tribune*, Orwell's friend, the writer and critic Julian Symons, catalogued several of these events in his life and concluded, "The particular quality that shines in his books was the ability to profit by such painful experiences, to put down aspects of his personal life, viewed with this peculiarly innocent eye, in direct and powerful prose." The essays in *Social Issues in Literature: The Abuse of Power in George Orwell's Nineteen Eighty-Four* trace Orwell's concern for the abuse of power in his novel as well as providing perspectives on the abuse of power today.

Chronology

1903

George Orwell is born Eric Arthur Blair on June 25 in Motihari, Bengal, India, the second child and only son of Richard Walmesley Blair and Ida Mabel Limouzin Blair.

1904

Ida Blair returns to England with her two children and settles in Henley-on-Thames while her husband remains in India.

1908–1911

Orwell attends Sunnylands, an Anglican school in Eastbourne, Sussex.

1911–1916

Orwell attends St. Cyprian's preparatory school in Eastbourne as a boarder.

1912

Richard Blair retires from the India Civil Service and returns home. The family moves to Shiplake, Oxfordshire, near Henley.

1914

Orwell publishes his first work, "Awake Young Men of England," a poem.

1915

The Blair family returns to Henley-on-Thames.

1917–1921

Narrowly missing a scholarship at Eton College, Orwell is accepted at Wellington College, where he spends the first nine weeks of 1917; however, a place opens for him at Eton College, and he transfers there in May as a King's Scholar.

1921

The Blair family moves to Southwold, Suffolk.

1922–1927

After passing an open examination, Orwell joins the Indian Imperial Police and serves as assistant superintendent of police in the force in Burma. His experiences cause him to develop a distaste for police work and to reject imperialism. He resigns while on leave in England in autumn of 1927, announces to his parents his intention to become a writer, and moves to the Notting Hill section of London.

1928–1929

Determined to become a writer, Orwell lives in Paris for eighteen months. He develops pneumonia and is hospitalized for two weeks in Spring 1929 at Hôpital Cochin.

1930–1931

Orwell returns to London and continues writing about social issues. He writes an early version of the autobiographical *Down and Out in Paris and London* and contributes "The Spike" and "The Hanging," two essays, to the journal *Adelphi* under his birth name.

1932–1933

Orwell teaches at the Hawthorns, a small private school in Hayes, Middlesex.

1933

Orwell's first book, *Down and Out in Paris and London*, is published by Victor Gollancz. It relates Orwell's experiences among the working class and poor in Paris and London. He teaches at Frays College, Uxbridge, Middlesex. In December, he is once more hospitalized with pneumonia.

1934

Orwell gives up teaching and spends ten months in Southwold. His first novel, *Burmese Days*, is published in the United States. He moves to Hampstead, London, in November and begins work in a bookshop. The bookshop is owned by members of the Independent Labour Party (ILP), a left-wing, anti-Communist party that Orwell joined in 1938.

1935

A Clergyman's Daughter is published. *Burmese Days* is published in England. Orwell meets Eileen O'Shaughnessy.

1936

At the suggestion of publisher Victor Gollancz, Orwell investigates working-class life and unemployment in Lancashire and Yorkshire, which results in the publication of *The Road to Wigan Pier* in 1937. Orwell and Eileen marry in June. *Keep the Aspidistra Flying* is published. He attends ILP Summer School, Letchworth, Hertsfordshire. In December, he goes to Spain to cover the Spanish Civil War as a journalist, then joins a combat unit to fight fascism.

1937

Involved in street fighting in Barcelona, Orwell is wounded in the throat by a sniper. He receives an honorable discharge for medical reasons. *The Road to Wigan Pier* is published.

1938

Orwell suffers a tubercular hemorrhage in his lung and is hospitalized in a sanitorium in Kent for six months. *Homage to Catalonia* is published. He joins the ILP. With his wife, Orwell travels to Morocco for his health.

1939

Orwell returns to England. *Coming Up for Air* is published. Richard Blair dies. The Hitler-Stalin Pact of August 1939 turns Orwell pro-war. He resigns from the pacifist ILP.

1940

Inside the Whale is published. Orwell moves to London and joins the Local Defense Volunteers (Home Guard). He writes reviews for *Time and Tide* and the *Tribune.*

1941

The Lion and the Unicorn is published. Orwell joins the British Broadcasting Company as talks producer and broadcaster to India. He writes reviews for the *Observer, Partisan Review,* and the *Manchester Evening News.*

1943

Ida Blair dies. Orwell becomes literary editor of the *Tribune.*

1944

The Orwells adopt a one-month old baby boy, whom they name Richard Horatio Blair.

1945

Orwell serves as a war correspondent for the *Observer* in Paris and Cologne. Eileen dies while under anesthetic during a minor operation. *Animal Farm* is published.

1946

Critical Essays is published. Orwell moves to the Isle of Jura in the Inner Hebrides to live with his son and a nurse in an abandoned farmhouse, where he begins work on *Nineteen Eighty-Four.*

1947

Orwell is hospitalized again with tuberculosis in Hairmyres Hospital, near Glasgow, Scotland.

1948

Orwell returns to Jura in July and completes *Nineteen Eighty-Four.*

1949

Orwell enters Cotswolds Sanitorium in Cranham, Gloucester-shire, and is then transferred to University College Hospital, London. *Nineteen Eighty-Four* is published in June and more than four hundred thousand copies are sold the first year. He marries Sonia Bronwell, an editorial assistant with *Horizon*, while in the hospital in October.

1950

Orwell dies suddenly in University College Hospital from a fatal hemorrhage on January 21. He is buried at the Church of All Saints, Sutton Courtenay, Oxfordshire.

Social Issues in Literature

CHAPTER 1

Background on George Orwell

The Life of George Orwell

David Morgan Zehr

David Morgan Zehr is a literary critic and English professor who taught at the University of Alabama.

In the following selection, Zehr explains that George Orwell was a complex figure whose vision united socialist political leanings with cultural and moral values that were conservative and conventional. Throughout his life, Orwell was distrustful of the left-wing intelligentsia and sympathetic to the common person. With Nineteen Eighty-Four, *Zehr states, Orwell wrote a novel that captured the anxieties of the Cold War era and added such terms as "Big Brother" and "doublethink" to the cultural vocabulary.*

George Orwell's remarkable international reputation is primarily due to his last two novels, *Animal Farm* (1945) and *Nineteen Eighty-Four* (1949), which have spoken to the Cold War consciousness with such force and intimacy that conceptions like Big Brother, "doublethink," and the apocalyptic date 1984 have become virtually mythic elements in our culture. Although Orwell became England's most prominent political writer during the 1940s, he was equally honored for his pragmatic, common-sensical habit of mind and for his uncompromising commitment to intellectual integrity. In fact, his career is a testimony to the enduring power of a moralist who tenaciously clings to the values of common decency, social justice, and respect for the individual. When Orwell died in January 1950, [British novelist and critic] V.S. Pritchett eulogized him as a "saint" and as the "conscience of his generation."

Orwell Championed the Common Man

Orwell was a complex, paradoxical figure who once described himself as a "Tory anarchist," a phrase which expressed his complex unification of radical and conservative impulses. Although he became a militant socialist after 1936, he was a fervent anticommunist and persistently attacked the "smelly little orthodoxies" which he felt had corrupted intellectual liberty. While he was committed to the power of the writer to influence and affect the direction of his society and its political order, he was convinced that ideological commitment would destroy the power of a writer: "To write in plain, vigorous language one has to think fearlessly, and if one thinks fearlessly one cannot be politically orthodox." He hated expediency (whether political or literary), sympathized with the poor and the underdog, opposed imperialism and aristocratic privilege, and became England's most vigorous spokesman for popular culture during the 1940s. He repeatedly defended the normative values of ordinary, bourgeois life, felt a persistent nostalgia for the order and stability of the pre-1914 world, and believed in the embryonic power within common, ordinary Englishmen. He became in the words of one writer, a "revolutionary patriot." Orwell's career—as novelist, essayist, and political pamphleteer—finally serves as a kind of barometer to an understanding of the conflicts and mood of the 1930s and 1940s and of the situation of the liberal writer working in a time of cultural and political crisis.

Middle-Class Origins

Eric Arthur Blair (he never legally changed his name to George Orwell) was born at Motihari in Bengal, India, on 25 June 1903, where his father was an undistinguished administrator in the Opium Department of the Government of India. He was the second child of Richard Walmsley and Ida Mabel Limouzin Blair. His mother returned to England with her children by 1905, although his father did not return permanently until 1911, when he retired. These early years in England, living at Henley-on-Thames, a very Edwardian town, would come to represent a period of happiness and security that affected Orwell's consciousness for the rest of his life. And yet he was also aware of conflicts. Years later he described himself as a member of the "lower-upper-middle class," a phrase which was meant to contrast the family's social rank (as servants of King and Country) with their middle-class economic status. Although the family was by no means impoverished, Orwell was later to insist that in this kind of "shabby-genteel family . . . there is far more *consciousness* of poverty than in any working-class family above the level of the dole." His awareness of having an ambivalent social position and of money's extraordinary importance would become prominent themes in Orwell's first four books and helped to shape his attitudes to what he came to see as the privileged intelligentsia.

In September 1911 he was sent to St. Cyprians, a snobbish and expensive private school, where he was to be prepared for entrance into one of the good public schools of England. The rigorous commitment to education and to the building of character at St. Cyprians was to make Orwell a promising candidate for public school, but the four years that he spent there also had a profound emotional impact on him, which he recorded in his posthumously published "Such, Such Were the Joys." This world was one in which money, position, and privilege seemed to be the determinate values, and Orwell came to feel like an alien in a foreign land. He remembers that the rich boys were openly favored and that he was reminded of his own tenuous economic status by being denied things because, he was told, his parents could not afford them. While a critic such as Anthony West finds the paradigm of the world of 1984 expressed in Orwell's recollections of favoritism, arbitrary rules, and the omnipotence of the system, it is perhaps more important to understand that during these years Orwell began to develop his antipathy toward authoritarian or institutionalized rule and began to develop an embryonic theory about victims and victimizers. This awareness of a fundamental conflict between the individual and a larger social structure would become an important social subject in his writing of the 1930s and a political subject in his work of the 1940s.

Educated at Eton

In the spring of 1916, Orwell sat for scholarship examinations for entrance into a public school. He narrowly missed a place at Eton but was accepted into Wellington, where he spent the first nine weeks of 1917; however, because of the war, a place opened up in the scholarship class at Eton, and in May 1917 he enrolled there. The atmosphere at Eton was much more open than at St. Cyprians: it was a freer intellectual environment, one in which individuality and intellectual freedom were encouraged. Orwell was later to say that the great virtue of the school was its "tolerant and civilized atmosphere which gives each boy a fair chance of developing his individuality." Immediately after the war Eton gained the reputation of being "Bolshie" [as in "Bolshevik"; i.e., politically left-wing]; there was a popular recoil against convention and authority, and Orwell's outspoken, cynical stance thrived in this atmosphere. Cyril Connolly, a contemporary at Eton, remembers that at the time Orwell rejected "the war, the Empire, [British author Rudyard] Kipling, Sussex, and Character." It was perhaps not unnatural that he should react against the values of his upbringing, education, and class, and yet, during these years, the values of patriotism, tradition, and tolerance were also deeply ingrained within him.

A Policeman in Burma

In December 1921 Orwell left Eton, but he suddenly felt displaced—both socially and psychologically. While the majority of his scholarship class went off to Oxford or Cambridge, there is no indication that Orwell wanted to go to the university nor is there any evidence that he felt any other particular sense of direction—including the desire to become a writer. While the Far East may have exerted a strong romantic pull for him (his father had been in India and he had a grandmother in Burma), his parents must have seen his relatively sudden decision to apply to the Indian Imperial Police as the logical consequence of his upbringing and family tradition. Early in 1922 he took the India Office examinations for the Indian Imperial Police and listed Burma as the first of his choices. On 27 October 1922 he sailed for Rangoon, Burma, where he was to be stationed as Assistant Superintendent of Police and to begin what would become a five-year interval between his Etonian skepticism and the beginning of his literary apprenticeship.

The effect of the Burmese experience on Orwell is difficult to gauge, but there is no indication that he found himself comfortable in an atmosphere in which the natives were hostile and the English jingoistic [aggressively patriotic]. The work was generally dull and routine, and Orwell is remembered as being solitary, unsocial, and eccentric. He apparently found the social-psychological pressures associated with being a British sahib [colonial lord] completely antithetical to the open intellectual environment at Eton, and this experience must have convinced him of the impossibility of accommodating himself to a conformist, establishment society. Perhaps another significant aspect of this five-year exile is that when he returned to England he had not yet read James Joyce, Marcel Proust, Virginia Woolf, Aldous Huxley, André Gide, T.S. Eliot, Ernest Hemingway, Ezra Pound, or any of the other major modernists who emerged during the second and third decades of the twentieth century. Prior to Burma he had been an enthusiastic reader, indulging himself mostly with William Thackeray, Charles Dickens, William Shakespeare, Rudyard Kipling, Jonathan Swift, G. Bernard Shaw, A.E. Houseman, Samuel Butler, and Somerset Maugham. When he returned to England his sensibility and literary imagination were not much different from what they were when he left England in 1922, and his early work was primarily influenced by his reading of Victorian and Edwardian writers.

Exploring Poverty in London

In August 1927 Orwell returned to England on leave. The following month he resigned his post and declared to his parents his intention of becoming a writer—a profession for which he had shown little inclination or promise up to that time. He moved to London in the autumn of 1927, and for the first time in his life he felt free from complex social pressures associated with his family, his schools, and his life in Burma—all of which had pressured him to adopt prescriptive codes of thought and behavior. The choice of becoming a writer, therefore, complexly involved the whole question of his social and psychological identity.

Early in 1928 Orwell put on some old rags and ventured into the East End of London in order to investigate the netherworld of the impoverished and unemployed. Why he voluntarily submerged himself into this underground world, which he had been taught to fear and despise, and continued to make such forays into it over the next three years, is not easy to answer. In 1936 he suggested that his quest for such experiences reflected the "bad conscience" he had when he returned from Burma: "I was conscious of an immense weight of guilt that I had got to expiate. . . . I felt that I had got to escape not merely from imperialism but from every form of man's dominion over man. I wanted to submerge myself, to get right down among the oppressed, to be one of them and on their side against their tyrants." While this explanation of the evolution of a socialist probably has its element of truth, it takes no account of his own adventurous spirit and says nothing about his motivation to become a writer or his attempt to break free from the bonds of his class and upbringing. Whatever the complex psychological reasons that drove Orwell to descend into the social abyss, these experiences proved to be formative in the shaping of his consciousness.

Living and Writing in Paris

In the spring of 1928 Orwell traveled to Paris, where he remained for eighteen months. Ostensibly he had gone there in order to live more cheaply than in London, but undoubtedly he was also drawn by the mystique of the bohemian, artistic life. However, while in Paris he showed a disciplined commitment to his late-chosen career. He had several articles published in Parisian newspapers, the subjects of which—unemployment, Burma, popular culture, political power, poverty, and social oppression—reflected what would continue to be his dominant interests. He also wrote two novels and a number of short stories, all of which were rejected. He returned to England at the end of 1929 and continued to write about his experiences. The first demonstrations that he was developing his own narrative voice are seen in "The Spike" and "A Hanging," which were published in *Adelphi* in 1931. What he had achieved for the first time with these two pieces was a successful blending of imaginative writing and reportage, and it was this fusion of two techniques that would give form to his first book.

The first version of *Down and Out in Paris and London* (1933) was completed in October 1930, initially titled "A Scullion's Diary." This early draft was written in the form of a diary and included only his Parisian experiences. The first publisher he submitted it to found it interesting but too short and fragmentary. Orwell then expanded it, adding the complementary section on London, altered the structure, and resubmitted it, only to have it rejected again. When T.S. Eliot, representing Faber and Faber, rejected it in February 1932, Orwell became severely dejected and began to look for a regular job.

In April 1932 he took a teaching position at The Hawthorns, in Hayes, Middlesex, a middle-class private school for boys (although he changed schools once, he continued to teach until December 1933). Finally, through the personal intervention of a friend, Orwell's manuscript was given to Victor Gollancz, who agreed to publish it. Orwell requested that it be brought out pseudonymously, and suggested four alternative names to Gollancz: P.S. Burton, Kenneth Miles, George Orwell, and H. Lewis Allways, and expressed a preference for George Orwell. Gollancz made the final decision on the name. The book was published on 9 January 1933, and the first printing sold out almost immediately and was followed by second and third printings. . . .

Early Novels Are Published

By December 1933 Orwell had finished his second book, *Burmese Days* (1934). Then, shortly before Christmas, 1933, he entered Uxbridge Cottage Hospital seriously ill with pneumonia (he later claimed that the climate of Burma had ruined his health), and after recovering he resigned his teaching position. He returned to his parents' home in Southwold in January 1934, where he began writing *A Clergyman's Daughter* (1935), which was completed by October of that year. He seems to have almost obsessively committed himself at this time to his writing and the formation of his career. He had some difficulty finding a publisher for *Burmese Days*. Victor Gollancz rejected it for fear of giving libelous offense to colonials in Burma and India. Harper and Brothers, in New York, after requesting some minor stylistic alterations, published it on 25 October 1934 (Gollancz finally brought this novel out in London in June 1935).

Burmese Days provides a finely drawn, convincing portrait of the provincial, chauvinistic British community in the small, backwater village of Kyauktada. . . .

In *A Clergyman's Daughter*, published on 11 March 1935, Orwell continued to examine the problematic relationship between an individual and a repressive, middle-class society that limits him with its rigid, exhausted values. This episodic novel tells the story of Dorothy Hare, the overworked only child of an acrimonious Church of England rector. Beset by both social and internal pressures that she is unable to cope with, Dorothy suffers a case of amnesia, which provides the vehicle for her escape from her hometown and her subsequent journeys into the hop fields of Kent, the social netherworld of London, and the lower-middle-class life of a fourth-rate private school. Orwell's own ambivalence in the novel is seen in the fact that he alternately sees Dorothy as his central subject, focusing on her crisis of self, and as a mere device for dramatizing his own experiences—he had also picked hops in Kent, been on the bum in London, been arrested (intentionally), and had taught in a private school. Although many of his works are strikingly autobiographical, this is one instance when he appears to have been more at the mercy of his material than in control of it. . . .

In October 1934 Orwell left his parents' home in Southwold and moved to Hampstead, on the outskirts of London, where he became a part-time assistant in a bookshop, Booklovers Corner. The bookshop was owned by the Westropes, who were members of the Independent Labour party (ILP), a left-wing, egalitarian, anticommunist, antimilitarist party that Orwell was to join in 1938. This period probably marks the beginning of his formal political education. He began *Keep the Aspidistra Flying* in February 1935, completed it by the end of the year, and it was published by Gollancz on 20 April 1936.

Gordon Comstock, the protagonist of *Keep the Aspidistra Flying*, is a struggling poet and an "angry young man" who believes that the modern world is dead and morally bankrupt and so gives up his job at an advertising agency, declares war on money, success, and all the bourgeois values associated with respectability, and takes a part-time job at a bookstore. He is a solipsistic hero whose festering bitterness and obsession with money overshadow the entire novel. Although he initially idealizes the bohemian life of the impoverished poet, his consciousness is still anchored in the money world, and he still accepts middle-class values. As a result he becomes caught up in a self-pitying, adolescent obsession with money that saps his personal energies and his ability to write and that disrupts his relationship with his girl friend, Rosemary. The novel attempts to identify Comstock's malaise with the decay and fatigue of his culture and provides some acute criticism of contemporary England, but it is difficult to believe that Comstock is anything but a petulant neurotic trapped in his own perverse consciousness. An uneven novel, it lacks the vigor, pace, and imaginative depth of his later writing. . . .

This novel is the first of Orwell's books in which we see the clear beginnings of his idealization of the ordinary in English life and of his commitment to traditional values. . . .

Marries and Fights in Spanish Civil War

Nineteen thirty-six was one of the pivotal years in Orwell's life. He married Eileen O'Shaughnessy on 9 June 1936. His relationship with this strong, independent woman (she was completing her M.A. in psychology) gave a new optimism and security to his life and very likely influenced the affirmative ending of *Keep the Aspidistra Flying*. In April 1936 he rented The Stores, a general store in Wallington, which he retained until 1939; when he was not writing, Orwell ran the store and took care of his garden and his goats. Until this time Orwell had remained curiously unaffected by the highly charged political atmosphere in England, but two significant experiences of 1936 fostered his transformation into a political writer. First, in January 1936 Victor Gollancz asked him to write a book on the conditions of the unemployed and the working class in the coal-mining districts of Yorkshire and Lancashire.

The resulting book, *The Road to Wigan Pier* (1937), contains his first clear identification with socialist aims and ideals. The second experience was his involvement in the Spanish Civil War, which began on 17 July 1936. Orwell went to Spain in December 1936 as a journalist, but almost immediately joined a combat unit in order to fight fascism. His experiences there deepened his commitment to socialism and produced a passionate distrust of the Communist party. This was probably the single most significant experience of his life, and it led him to write in 1947: "Every line of serious work that I have written since 1936 has been written, directly or indirectly, *against* totalitarianism and *for* democratic Socialism, as I understand it." However, Gollancz felt compelled to add a critical foreword to *The Road to Wigan Pier*, taking issue with Orwell's unorthodox socialism, and refused to publish *Homage to Catalonia* because of what he saw as its heretical political point of view, suggesting the degree to which Orwell was outside the dominant mainstream of leftist politics during the mid-1930s. He was on his way to becoming not only an important socialist writer, but to becoming a morally committed dissident in an age that had become infatuated with orthodoxy. . . .

When Orwell came to write *Homage to Catalonia* (published 25 April 1938), he set out to write not a history of the war or a political documentary but a personal memoir that would chronicle his subjective experience of the drudgery of war, of a social revolution, and of an interparty political conflict. In so doing he was able to successfully transform the documentary into both a descriptive and an expressive form that has made this one of Orwell's most popular books. Although his involvement in Spain was relatively short (December 1936–June 1937), it profoundly influenced the direction and shape of his personal and literary imagination. The disillusionment and anger that he felt over the dubious, self-serving role of the Communist party in Spain, and over what he saw of the extensive rewriting of history for the purposes of propaganda and deception, provided the seminal experiences that would inform and structure *Animal Farm* and *Nineteen Eighty-Four*. And yet, his experiences of comradeship and community in Spain furthered his belief in the essential goodness and potential power of the common people—and the vigor, buoyancy, and elan with which *Homage to Catalonia* is written testifies to the personal significance of these experiences. . . .

Back on the Aragon front [in Spain], Orwell was wounded through the neck on 20 May 1937; one of his vocal cords was damaged, leaving his voice altered for the rest of his life. When he returned to Barcelona in June the POUM [Workers Party of Marxist Unification, of which he had become a member,] had been outlawed, and he lived like a fugitive, sleeping in deserted churches and parks at night, until he and his wife (she had come to Barcelona in February to work at the ILP office) managed to cross the border into France, after a number of his comrades had already been arrested. If Orwell had gone to Spain to fight against fascism, he returned with a more complex understanding of power politics, and with the recognition that it was totalitarianism that was a threat to the liberty of Europe and to England's liberal heritage. . . .

Develops Tuberculosis

In March 1938 a turbercular lesion on one lung began to hemorrhage, and be spent five months in a sanatorium. During Orwell's period of recovery the novelist L.H. Meyers anonymously gave him £300 so that he could go to Morocco for his health. He and Eileen left in September 1938 for Marrakesh, where he wrote *Coming Up for Air*. They returned to London in the spring of 1939.

Coming Up for Air (published on 12 June 1939) is narrated by George Bowling, a middle-aged, nonintellectual, lower-middle-class insurance salesman who is acutely responsive to the political insecurities of 1938. As we might expect, the novel is permeated with a sense of the inevitability of the coming war and the horrors that will accompany it, and yet much of the power of the novel is derived from its counter-pointing of the pre-1914 world in which Bowling grew up with the acute contemporaneity of the world of 1938....

The outbreak of war in 1939 intensified Orwell's feelings of anxiety and pessimism. In his finest essay of the 1930s, "Inside the Whale," completed shortly after the start of the war, he exhibited a sharply accelerating tone of pessimism and near hysteria: "The literature of liberalism is coming to an end and the literature of totalitarianism has not yet appeared and is barely imaginable...."

World War II Intensifies Orwell's Patriotism

The war influenced him in another significant way: while he developed a growing antipathy toward politics, his militant antiwar stance of 1938–1939 yielded now to an equally militant patriotism. He tried several times to enlist in military service, but was turned down because of his precarious health (lesions on his lung). He found an outlet for his patriotism and for his continuing revolutionary feelings through two means: first, he joined the Home Guard in June 1940 (serving as a sergeant until November 1943), and second, he began to formulate what can only be called a "myth" of an English cultural heritage, which embodied both his patriotism and his faith in the potential power of the common, ordinary Englishmen. While this "myth" probably has its beginnings in *Coming Up for Air*, he sets it forth in "May Country Right or Left" (1940), in which he defines patriotism as a "devotion to something that is changing but [which] is felt to be mystically the same," and then develops it more complexly in his pamphlet *The Lion and the Unicorn; Socialism and the English Genius* (1941)....

In August 1941 he finally found "essential service" by joining the BBC as Talks Assistant (later as Talks Producer) in the

Indian section of its Eastern Service, where he remained until November 1943. While at the BBC he witnessed a great deal of propaganda (from both sides), which served to heighten his fears that the concept of objective truth was fading out of the world. . . . When he resigned from the BBC in November 1943, he joined the *Tribune* as literary editor, and began writing *Animal Farm*. Also, in June 1943, he and Eileen adopted a baby, whom they named Richard Horatio Blair.

Animal Farm Becomes a Best Seller

Animal Farm was written between November 1943 and February 1944, but was not published until August 1945, principally as a result of political objections that arose over the book's attack on [Joseph] Stalin and the Soviet Union. It was turned down by a number of publishers in England (including T.S. Eliot at Faber and Faber) and America. One American publisher rejected it because, he said, Americans were not in the mood for animal stories. Orwell, fearing implicit censorship and convinced of the urgency of his message, considered publishing it himself as a two-shilling pamphlet. Finally, Secker and Warburg agreed to publish it, but it was still held for publication until the end of the war, ostensibly because of lack of paper, but more likely because it was still deemed imprudent to publish something attacking the Soviet Union when it was a valuable ally of the West. When the novel was finally published the magnitude of its success surprised Orwell as much as anyone. The first edition sold out the first month, and by the spring of 1946 it was being translated into nine languages. After the Book-of-the-Month Club in America chose it as a selection, it sold more than a half-million copies, relieving him from financial worries for the first time in his life.

The specific political purpose that had aroused Orwell's sense of urgency was his desire to explode the myth of the Soviet Union as the paradigm of the socialist state. He also wanted to expose the dangers of totalitarianism, which he saw reflected in the politics of expedience, the devaluation of objective truth, and the systematic manipulation of the common people through propaganda. . . .

Although by 1945 Orwell had achieved an international reputation and relative economic security, his last years continued to be wrought with tension. In the spring of 1945 he resigned from his job as literary editor at the *Tribune* and traveled to Europe as a war correspondent. While he was in Europe his wife died on 29 March 1945 during an operation apparently for cancer. Later in that year he became vice chairman of the Freedom Defense Committee, which was headed by Herbert Read and which was established in order to fight for civil liberties. In February 1946 Secker and Warburg published a collection of his finest essays, *Critical Essays* (published in the United States as *Dickens, Dali and Others*). He had been dreaming since the early 1940s about the possibility of escaping to an island in the Hebrides (off Scotland), where he could garden and have sufficient peace to work; and in May 1946 he finally rented a house on Jura, in the Outer Hebrides, where he lived until shortly before his death. It was there that he wrote most of *Nineteen Eighty-Four* (he had been making notes for his final work since 1944, and had originally entitled it "The Last Man in Europe"), completing the first draft in October 1947. Two months later his tuberculosis again forced him into a sanatorium, where he spent seven months, unable to work for the majority of that time. He returned to Jura at the end of July 1948, where he completed *Nineteen Eighty-Four*. The book was published on 5 June 1949, and in its first year sold some 45,000 copies in England and over 170,000 copies in America.

In *Nineteen Eighty-Four* Orwell envisions a time in the near future when the world has been divided into three super states, each of which is ruled by a system of oligarchical collectivism that has brutally eliminated privacy, intellectual freedom, friendship, and the autonomy of the individual, and each of which has systematically deprived its inhabitants of a verifiable history and of the resources of a cultural consciousness. It is a mistake to read this work as a fatalistic prophecy of the death of civilization, for Orwell's primary purpose is to magnify and distort disturbing conditions, tendencies, and habits of thought that he saw existing in the world, so that they could be recognized and arrested. . . .

Dies of Tuberculosis

Despite Orwell's continued preoccupation with politics and with the fate of his civilization, in the last years of his life he was planning long essays on [Joseph] Conrad, [George] Gissing, and [Evelyn] Waugh—suggesting his renewed interest in the traditional forms of the novel. Laurence Brander reports that during the closing months of his life Orwell was "ready to turn from politics and polemics to the normal preoccupation of the literary artist in our time, the study of human relationship." On 13 October 1949 he married Sonia Brownell, whom he had known for about five years, and on 21 January 1950 he died of tuberculosis at the University of London Hospital, at the age of forty-six.

Although his experiences and the temper of his age transformed George Orwell into a political writer, he never ceased to affirm the value of a nonideological tradition of the novel and to celebrate the normative values of English cultural life. Indeed, he remained committed to a manifestly liberal tradition of the artist: he continued to see art as a means of enlarging man's sympathies and testifying to his humanity and to see the writer as a central social intelligence, capable of affecting human awareness, transmitting moral values, influencing the order and direction of his society, and celebrating the values and vitality of the common, ordinary man. And it is for these reasons, and not simply because of his last two novels, that Orwell continues to speak to us with so much vigor and clarity.

Orwell Sees No Contradiction Between Patriotism and Socialism

George Orwell

Eric Blair, under the pen name George Orwell, was a British novelist, journalist, and essayist and an influential political writer with socialist views. His best-known novels, Animal Farm *and* Nineteen Eighty-Four, *parody life in Soviet Russia and foretell a totalitarian future, respectively.*

In the following selection Orwell describes his feelings of patriotism during World War II. He contends that there is no contradiction between being patriotic to one's country and still believing that that country can have a better government. Orwell describes a visceral, emotional desire to support his country that has its roots in his upbringing and his culture.

Contrary to popular belief, the past was not more eventful than the present. If it seems so it is because when you look backward things that happened years apart are telescoped together, and because very few of your memories come to you genuinely virgin. It is largely because of the books, films and reminiscences that have come between that the war of 1914–18 is now supposed to have had some tremendous, epic quality that the present one lacks.

But if you were alive during that war, and if you disentangle your real memories from their later accretions, you find that it was not usually the big events that stirred you at the

George Orwell, "My Country Right or Left," in *The Collected Essays, Journalism and Letters of George Orwell: Volume I: An Age Like This, 1920-1940*, eds. Sonia Orwell and Ian Angus. Copyright © George Orwell, 1968, renewed 1996 by Mark Hamiilton. Reproduced by permission of Bill Hamilton as the Literary Executor of the Estate of the Late Sonia Brownwell Orwell, Secker & Warburg Ltd., and Houghton Mifflin Harcourt Publishing Company.

time. I don't believe that the Battle of the Marne, for instance, had for the general public the melodramatic quality that it was afterwards given. I do not even remember hearing the phrase "Battle of the Marne" till years later. It was merely that the Germans were 22 miles from Paris—and certainly that was terrifying enough, after the Belgian atrocity stories—and then for some reason they had turned back. I was eleven when the war started. If I honestly sort out my memories and disregard what I have learned since, I must admit that nothing in the whole war moved me so deeply as the loss of the *Titanic* had done a few years earlier. This comparatively petty disaster shocked the whole world, and the shock has not quite died away even yet. I remember the terrible, detailed accounts read out at the breakfast table (in those days it was a common habit to read the newspaper aloud), and I remember that in all the long list of horrors the one that most impressed me was that at the last the *Titanic* suddenly up-ended and sank bow foremost, so that the people clinging to the stern were lifted no less than three hundred feet into the air before they plunged into the abyss. It gave me a sinking sensation in the belly which I can still all but feel. Nothing in the war ever gave me quite that sensation.

Of the outbreak of war I have three vivid memories which, being petty and irrelevant, are uninfluenced by anything that has come later. One is of the cartoon of the "German Emperor" (I believe the hated name "Kaiser" was not popularised till a little later) that appeared in the last days of July. People were mildly shocked by this guying of royalty ("But he's such a handsome man, really!"), although we were on the edge of war. Another is of the time when the army commandeered all the horses in our little country town, and a cabman burst into tears in the market-place when his horse, which had worked for him for years, was taken away from him. And another is of a mob of young men at the railway station, scrambling for the evening papers that had just arrived on the London train. And

I remember the pile of peagreen papers (some of them were still green in those days), the high collars, the tightish trousers and the bowler hats, far better than I can remember the names of the terrific battles that were already raging on the French frontier.

Of the middle years of the war, I remember chiefly the square shoulders, bulging calves and jingling spurs of the artillerymen, whose uniform I much preferred to that of the infantry. As for the final period, if you ask me to say truthfully what is my chief memory, I must answer simply—margarine. It is an instance of the horrible selfishness of children that by 1917 the war had almost ceased to affect us, except through our stomachs. In the school library a huge map of the Western Front was pinned on an easel, with a red silk thread running across on a zig-zag of drawing-pins. Occasionally the thread moved half an inch this way or that, each movement meaning a pyramid of corpses. I paid no attention. I was at school among boys who were above the average level of intelligence, and yet I do not remember that a single major event of the time appeared to us in its true significance. The Russian Revolution, for instance, made no impression, except on the few whose parents happened to have money invested in Russia. Among the very young the pacifist reaction had set in long before the war ended. To be as slack as you dared on OTC parades, and to take no interest in the war, was considered a mark of enlightenment. The young officers who had come back, hardened by their terrible experience and disgusted by the attitude of the younger generation to whom this experience meant just nothing, used to lecture us for our softness. Of course they could produce no argument that we were capable of understanding. They could only bark at you that war was "a good thing", it "made you tough", "kept you fit", etc etc. We merely sniggered at them. Ours was the one-eyed pacifism that is peculiar to sheltered countries with strong navies. For years after the war, to have any knowledge of or interest in military matters, even to know which end of a gun the bullet comes out of, was suspect in "enlightened" circles. 1914–18 was written off as a meaningless slaughter, and even the men who had been slaughtered were held to be in some way to blame. I have often laughed to think of that recruiting poster, "What did you do in the Great War, daddy?" (a child is asking this question of its shame-stricken father), and of all the men who must have been lured into the army by just that poster and afterwards despised by their children for not being Conscientious Objectors.

But the dead men had their revenge after all. As the war fell back into the past, my particular generation, those who had been "just too young", became conscious of the vastness of the experience they had missed. You felt yourself a little less than a man, because you had missed it. I spent the years 1922–7 mostly among men a little older than myself who had been through the war. They talked about it unceasingly, with horror, of course, but also with a steadily growing nostalgia. You can see this nostalgia perfectly clearly in the English war-books. Besides, the pacifist reaction was only a phase, and even the "just too young" had all been trained for war. Most of the English middle class are trained for war from the cradle onwards, not technically but morally. The earliest political slogan I can remember is "We want eight (eight dreadnoughts) and we won't wait". At seven years old I was a member of the Navy League and wore a sailor suit with "HMS *Invincible*" on my cap. Even before my public-school OTC I had been in a private-school cadet corps. On and off, I have been toting a rifle ever since I was ten, in preparation not only for war but for a particular kind of war, a war in which the guns rise to a frantic orgasm of sound, and at the appointed moment you clamber out of the trench, breaking your nails on the sandbags, and stumble across mud and wire into the machine-gun barrage. I am convinced that part of the reason for the fascination that the Spanish civil war had for people of about my

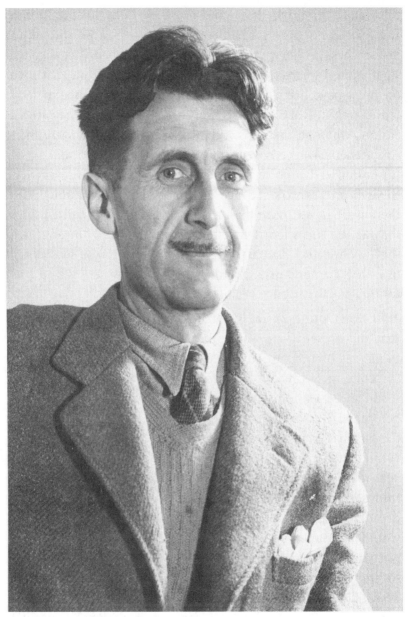

Author George Orwell, who explores government's abuse of power in his novel Nineteen Eighty-Four. AP Images.

age was that it was so like the Great War. At certain moments Franco was able to scrape together enough aeroplanes to raise the war to a modern level, and these were the turning-points. But for the rest it was a bad copy of 1914–18, a positional war of trenches, artillery, raids, snipers, mud, barbed wire, lice and stagnation. In early 1937 the bit of the Aragon front that I was on must have been very like a quiet sector in France in 1915. It was only the artillery that was lacking. Even on the rare occasions when all the guns in Huesca and outside it were firing simultaneously, there were only enough of them to make a fitful unimpressive noise like the ending of a thunderstorm. The shells from Franco's six-inch guns crashed loudly enough, but there were never more than a dozen of them at a time. I know that what I felt when I first heard artillery fired "in anger", as they say, was at least partly disappointment. It was so different from the tremendous, unbroken roar that my senses had been waiting for for twenty years.

I don't quite know in what year I first knew for certain that the present war was coming. After 1930, of course, the thing was obvious to anyone except an idiot. For several years the coming war was a nightmare to me, and at times I even made speeches and wrote pamphlets against it. But the night before the Russo-German pact was announced I dreamed that the war had started. It was one of those dreams which, whatever Freudian inner meaning they may have, do sometimes reveal to you the real state of your feelings. It taught me two things, first, that I should be simply relieved when the long-dreaded war started, secondly, that I was patriotic at heart, would not sabotage or act against my own side, would support the war, would fight in it if possible. I came downstairs to find the newspaper announcing Ribbentrop's flight to Moscow.[1] So war was coming, and the Government, even the Chamberlain Government, was assured of my loyalty. Needless to say this loyalty was and remains merely a gesture. As with almost everyone I know, the Government has flatly refused to

1. On 21 August 1939 Ribbentrop was invited to Moscow and on 23 August he and Molotov signed the Russo-German Pact.

employ me in any capacity whatever, even as a clerk or a private soldier. But that does not alter one's feelings. Besides, they will be forced to make use of us sooner or later.

If I had to defend my reasons for supporting the war, I believe I could do so. There is no real alternative between resisting Hitler and surrendering to him, and from a Socialist point of view I should say that it is better to resist; in any case I can see no argument for surrender that does not make nonsense of the Republican resistance in Spain, the Chinese resistance to Japan, etc etc. But I don't pretend that that is the emotional basis of my actions. What I knew in my dream that night was that the long drilling in patriotism which the middle classes go through had done its work, and that once England was in a serious jam it would be impossible for me to sabotage. But let no one mistake the meaning of this. Patriotism has nothing to do with conservatism. It is devotion to something that is changing but is felt to be mystically the same, like the devotion of the ex-White Bolshevik to Russia. To be loyal both to Chamberlain's England and to the England of tomorrow might seem an impossibility, if one did not know it to be an everyday phenomenon. Only revolution can save England, that has been obvious for years, but now the revolution has started, and it may proceed quite quickly if only we can keep Hitler out. Within two years, maybe a year, if only we can hang on, we shall see changes that will surprise the idiots who have no foresight. I dare say the London gutters will have to run with blood. All right, let them, if it is necessary. But when the red militias are billeted in the Ritz I shall still feel that the England I was taught to love so long ago and for such different reasons is somehow persisting.

I grew up in an atmosphere tinged with militarism, and afterwards I spent five boring years within the sound of bugles. To this day it gives me a faint feeling of sacrilege not to stand to attention during "God Save the King". That is childish, of course, but I would sooner have had that kind of upbringing than be like the left-wing intellectuals who are so "enlight-ened" that they cannot understand the most ordinary emo-tions. It is exactly the people whose hearts have *never* leapt at the sight of Union Jack who will flinch from revolution when the moment comes. Let anyone compare the poem John Corn-ford wrote not long before he was killed ("Before the Storm-ing of Huesca") with Sir Henry Newbolt's "There's a breathless hush in the Close tonight". Put aside the technical differences, which are merely a matter of period, and it will be seen that the emotional content of the two poems is almost exactly the same. The young Communist who died heroically in the In-ternational Brigade was public school to the core. He had changed his allegiance but not his emotions. What does that prove? Merely the possibility of building a Socialist on the bones of a Blimp, the power of one kind of loyalty to trans-mute itself into another, the spiritual need for patriotism and the military virtues, for which, however little the boiled rab-bits of the Left may like them, no substitute has yet been found.

Orwell Was Highly Principled

V.S. Pritchett

V.S. Pritchett was a British novelist, educator, essayist, and critic. Among his many books is the well-known Midnight Oil.

In this obituary of George Orwell, Pritchett celebrates the two sides of the writer—the socialist who called attention to the plight of suffering humanity and the humanist who celebrated the simple pleasures of a pastoral existence.

George Orwell was the wintry conscience of a generation which in the 'thirties had heard the call to the rasher assumptions of political faith. He was a kind of saint and, in that character, more likely in politics to chasten his own side than the enemy. His instinctive choice of spiritual and physical discomfort, his habit of going his own way, looked like the crankishness which has often cropped up in the British character; if this were so, it was vagrant rather than puritan. He prided himself on seeing through the rackets, and on conveying the impression of living without the solace or even the need of a single illusion.

Two George Orwells

There can hardly have been a more belligerent and yet more pessimistic Socialist; indeed his Socialism became anarchism. In corrupt and ever worsening years, he always woke up one miserable hour earlier than anyone else and, suspecting something fishy in the site, broke camp and advanced alone to some tougher position in a bleaker place; and it had often happened that he had been the first to detect an unpleasant truth or to refuse a tempting hypocrisy. Conscience took the Anglo-Indian out of the Burma police, conscience sent the old

V.S. Pritchett, "George Orwell," *New Statesman and Nation*, January 28, 1950, p. 96.

Etonian among the down and outs in London and Paris, and the degraded victims of the Means Test [a test to determine eligibility for public assistance] or slum incompetence in Wigan [a mill town in Manchester, England]; it drove him into the Spanish civil war and, inevitably, into one of its unpopular sects, and there Don Quixote saw the poker face of Communism. His was the guilty conscience of the educated and privileged man, one of that regular supply of brilliant recalcitrants which Eton has given us since the days of [author Henry] Fielding; and this conscience could be allayed only by taking upon itself the pain, the misery, the dinginess and the pathetic but hard vulgarities of a stale and hopeless period.

But all this makes only the severe half of George Orwell's character. There were two George Orwells even in name. I see a tall emaciated man with a face scored by the marks of physical suffering. There is the ironic grin of pain at the ends of kind lips, and an expression in the fine eyes that had something of the exalted and obstructive farsightedness one sees in the blind; an expression that will suddenly become gentle, lazily kind and gleaming with workmanlike humour. He would be jogged into remembering mad, comical and often tender things which his indignation had written off; rather like some military man taking time off from a private struggle with the War Office or society in general.

He was an expert in living on the bare necessities and a keen hand at making them barer. There was a sardonic suggestion that he could do this but you could not. He was a handyman. He liked the idea of a bench. I remember once being advised by him to go in for goat-keeping, partly I think because it was a sure road to trouble and semi-starvation; but as he set out the alluring disadvantages, it seemed to dawn on him that he was arguing for some country Arcadia [mythic place of peace and pastoral simplicity], some Animal Farm, he had once known; goats began to look like escapism and, turning aside as we walked to buy some shag at a struggling [H.G.]

Wellsian small trader's shop, he switched the subject sharply to the dangerous Fascist tendencies of the St John's Wood Home Guard who were marching to imaginary battle under the Old School Tie [network of graduates of the same school].

Future in the Hands of the Working Class

As an Old School Tie himself, Orwell had varied one of its traditions and had 'gone native' in his own country. It is often said that he knew nothing about the working classes, and indeed a certain self-righteousness in the respectable working class obviously repelled his independent mind. So many of his contemporaries had 'gone native' in France; he redressed a balance. But he did know that sour, truculent, worrying, vulgar lower class England of people half 'done down,' commercially exploited, culturally degraded, lazy, feckless, mild and kind who had appear in the novels of [Charles] Dickens, were to show their heads again in Wells and now stood in danger of having the long Victorian decency knocked out of them by gangster politics.

By 'the people' he did not mean what the politicians mean; but he saw, at least in his Socialist pamphlets, that it was they who would give English life of the future a raw, muddy but unmistakable and inescapable flavour. His masochism, indeed, extended to culture.

In a way, he deplored this. A classical education had given him a taste for the politician who can quote from [the Roman poet] Horace; and as was shown in the lovely passages of boyhood reminiscence in *Coming Up for Air*, his imagination was full only in the kind world he had known before 1914. Growing up turned him not exactly into a misanthrope—he was too good-natured and spirited for that—but into one who felt too painfully the ugly pressure of society, upon private virtue and happiness. His own literary tastes were fixed—with a discernible trailing of the coat—in that boyish period: Bret Harte, Jules Verne, pioneering stuff, [Rudyard] Kipling and boys' books. He wrote the best English appreciation of Dickens of our time. *Animal Farm* has become a favourite book for children. His Burmese novels, though poor in character, turn Kipling upside down. As a reporting pamphleteer, his fast, clear, grey prose carries its hard and sweeping satire perfectly.

He has gone; but in one sense, he always made this impression of the passing traveller who meets one on the station, points out that one is waiting for the wrong train and vanishes. His popularity, after *Animal Farm*, must have disturbed such a lone hand. In *1984*, alas, one can see that deadly pain, which had long been his subject, had seized him completely and obliged him to project a nightmare, as Wells had done in his last days, upon the future.

Orwell Was Morally Right on Major Issues

Christopher Hitchens

Named by Forbes *magazine in 2009 as one of the twenty-five most influential liberals in the U.S. media, Christopher Hitchens is a British-born author, journalist, literary critic, and political commentator and writer. He is the author of* God Is Not Great: How Religion Poisons Everything.

In the following selection Hitchens asserts that George Orwell remains relevant today because of the compelling nature of his writing—he avoided the trite and wrote memorable phrases. Nineteen Eighty-Four *has the ring of truth to it, Hitchens claims, because Orwell put into it his own personal experiences with brutality—at an authoritarian boys school, as a police officer in Burma, and during the Spanish Civil War. According to Hitchens, although Orwell got some of the details wrong, he was morally right on the three major questions of his day—imperialism, fascism, and communism.*

George Orwell didn't make it into 1950 before expiring. Nonetheless, his identity thereafter has been subject to theft and appropriation. His essay on [Charles] Dickens begins by saying, "Dickens is a writer worth stealing." Orwell is closer in time and in some ways in life to Dickens than we are to Orwell. And Orwell died, in a sense, a Dickensian death. He died partly of poverty, ill health, neglect, and the unavailability of drugs that he could have had if he had been better informed. He lived to be forty-six in the twentieth century and yet as we enter the twenty-first century there must be a good answer as to why we are so preoccupied with him....

A Masterly Writer

There is a reason to pay tribute to Orwell. When some of us invoke the name of George Orwell in contemporary politics for contemporary reasons we do so not in the hope of acquiring his reputation for honesty and courage. After all, a moment's thought will tell you that I can lay no such claim. And no one would believe me if I tried to emulate someone who took such risks and was willing to endure such hardship for his convictions. There's another reason, which I would describe as a literary reason, why Orwell remains alive to us. His favorite texts, ones that he could usually quote from memory and often did so with very small mistakes, were the canonical works of William Shakespeare, the prayer book of Archbishop [Thomas] Cranmer, and the King James Bible. Those texts too contain phrases, thoughts, simple offhand descriptions that come to us when we need them, that stay in our cortexes because of the exquisite care with which they were composed. No one saying "I do not believe that the powers that be are ordained of God" is expecting to have it believed by the audience that he has made up this term himself or is claiming the mantle of St. Paul. He is arguing about a proposition, the wording of which everybody knows. And in my view, the reason for the enduring legacy of Orwell is precisely that. And here's the contradiction: when we try to struggle against totalitarianism, not just as a system or a threat but in our own minds and the bad habits it inculcates, we also strive to avoid the obvious. We strive to avoid catch-phrases and stale phrases. Orwell pointed out two beauties I remember offhand about Nazism: the jackboot has been thrown into the melting pot, and on another occasion: the fascist octopus has sung its swan song. The people who use slogans of this kind have ceased to think about the meaning of words. These are examples of what the French used to call the *langue du bois*—the wooden tongue. Claud Cockburn, Orwell's great enemy and great antagonist in Spain and father of Orwell's leading critic in the

United States, when he worked for the *Daily Worker* saw that one article in the magazine in a communiqué from Moscow said that the leading organs of the party should begin to penetrate the backward parts of the proletariat. In response, the editors said, "that's from Moscow, you can't change that." The fear that people have not just of recognizing totalitarianism as a threat or calling evil by its right name arises in part because if these threats are true and if these evils are existent, they themselves may be called upon to witness or to fight or to do something about it.

There is an element of denial in the refusal to admit that the threat has arisen in the first place. Orwell puts one on one's guard against that tendency to euphemism and he does it in phrases that are memorable and that are drawn from the great wellsprings of English writing. His atheism was Protestant, in other words. He believed that the struggle for a Bible that was in English and understood by the people was a great struggle for free speech and that the inner part, the priesthood, should never possess or have exclusive claim on what was sacred in order to make it more profane. . . .

Personal Experiences of Totalitarianism

Author to author tributes are not that refulgent sometimes and not that common. I would nominate as the greatest compliment made from one author to another the remark made by Czelaw Milosz in his book *The Captive Mind*, which was written in 1951 and published in the West in 1953. Milosz was then a cultural official of the Polish communist regime, but he had begun internally to dissent and to compose the essays that make up *The Captive Mind*, which is a book that bears extensive rereading. And Milosz wrote, about the moral and political atmosphere of [Joseph] Stalin's Warsaw, the following:

> A few have become acquainted with Orwell's *1984*; because it is both difficult to obtain and dangerous to possess, it is known only to certain members of the Inner Party. Orwell

fascinates them through his insight into details they know well and through his use of [Jonathan] Swiftian satire. Such a form of writing is forbidden by the New Faith because allegory, by nature manifold in meaning, would trespass beyond the prescriptions of socialist realism and the demands of the censor. Even those who know Orwell only by hearsay are amazed that a writer that never lived in Russia should have so keen a perception into its life.

Now think about that. Orwell died as he was finishing, and seeing into the press, *Nineteen Eighty-Four*. He never saw it become a success. It describes a party regime where the inner party possesses a secret book that may possibly tell them what the truth of the matter is. Within two years in Stalin's Warsaw, the man who is now accepted by all as the great national literary laureate of Poland but was then a struggling member of the bureaucracy writes that there is a book within the Polish inner party that has circulated and that is *Nineteen Eighty-Four*. This is an extraordinary tribute and I think an unparalleled one. And I want to comment quickly on why I think Milosz was slightly wrong. In fact, Orwell had understood and had had the experience of living in a totalitarian society. In a very small way, and I don't mean this to sound flippant, in a very small way he had had it by being at a very authoritarian, bullying, and sadistic little boy's school that he described as a tender lad in his wonderful essay "Such, Such Were the Joys." I've had the experience of being at such a school at the same age. I was luckier than he was, but not by that much. I remember thinking it was good preparation for living in extreme times. The experience was not wasted on him. The way in which people will betray one another. The way in which power and cruelty can exert a pull of attraction, not just fear, upon those upon whom it is exerted. He had been a policeman in colonial Burma and had worked out that there is a dirty secret at the heart of power. There's a dirty secret and it is this: The most qualified Indian or Burmese person would never get, if he was a man, into the English club no matter how well he spoke English and no matter how many degrees and qualifications he had. He would never be admitted by the front door, even as a guest. But the most un-qualified Burmese girl could he admitted to the villa of the British official as long as it was by the back door and as long as money changed hands.

Indeed in *Burmese Days*, Orwell describes a police of-ficer—clearly himself—as having bought his Burmese mistress from her family. I believe myself that he resigned from the service of the police because he was afraid that if he kept on with it he would become a sadist and robot and someone governed by racial prejudice. He understood that, and he had also seen a political witch hunt and a show trial and a reign of terror in Catalonia in Barcelona during the Spanish Civil War. In fact, he had seen two reigns of terror—one from the fascist side and one from the communist side.

Milosz did not know that this was so. All he knew was that some Englishman had captured the moral atmosphere of Stalin's Europe without living there. But there are ingredients that went into *Nineteen Eighty-Four* and these are the insights that I think are very unlikely to become tedious to us or un-worthy of further consideration. These are not, in other words, historical considerations: they are alarmingly contemporary. And on top of these experiences—because many people had the experience of both brutality and brutalization, which are not, as you know, the same thing—Orwell had an instinct for language. He wrote that he knew from the start, as soon as he read the first pamphlet and the first proclamation from the USSR, that by the language you could tell that something hid-eous was being done there. Actually, you could be tipped off pretty easily. Anything that is called a great "experiment" is going to be pretty nasty because we don't use humans for ex-periments and we don't, on the whole, respect people who do. Always attend to the language. He didn't have to visit, in other

In the Gothic Quarter of Barcelona, Spain, a plaça (plaza) is named in honor of George Orwell, who fought against fascist forces in the Spanish Civil War from 1936 to 1937. © Paul Taylor/Alamy.

words, even though he had ancillary and corollary experience. By the language he could tell what was filthy and dangerous and mean and doomed about this system. So he got the three greatest issues of the twentieth century right in part because he got other things wrong.

Orwell Was Morally Right

I want to talk a little bit about the essential nature of contradiction in this subject. I'll try and materialize the contradiction. You can as a pedantic matter say that Orwell got right the three great questions of empire, fascism, and Stalinism and he did it quite early. Quite early in the 1920s, he saw that the Englishman's day in India and Burma was done. And that was a struggle with himself. So was the struggle to expose the great lie of communism among his intellectual friends, not just as an illusion but as a delusion, a falsehood, a foul propaganda that should be exposed, not pitied. And then about the struggle against fascism. When I talk about struggle within himself, I mean this: Orwell was born into a family that helped run the drug trade. His father was involved in the British colonial business of forcing China to buy opium made in India. That's why Orwell later refers to British society as a family where there is a terrible conspiracy of silence about the source of family income. That's why he never mentions his father or a father figure in anything he writes, only a big brother. He was brought up to dislike and despise Jewish people. He was brought up to distrust the great unwashed and the proletarians and the masses. If he wasn't brought up to be misogynistic, his upbringing was enough to make him very suspicious and fearful of women. And for reasons we may never fully understand, he was evidently very distraught at the mention of male homosexuality.

So how right, really, was Orwell on the three main questions? On empire he was wrong. He believed it was merely a racket. He thought that the British people would be poorer if India and the colonies were given up. That the English people would have to live on potatoes and herrings if they didn't exploit the colonies. He knew nothing about investment, trade, and innovation in the imperial economy. But he was morally right in that he saw that the white man's day was done, that there was no God-given right for European countries to run as their property Africa, India and other underdeveloped regions. And he was very right in his contemporary challenge to the chauvinism of the British labor movement (there was at least someone more exploited than themselves).

On fascism, Orwell barely wrote anything. He seems to have assumed that nobody needed to be persuaded about fascism. At one point he did say that fascism was indistinguishable from democracy and plutocracy. And several times he said that imperialism was worse than fascism. He was wrong about it, in other words, while being right. He was morally right. In the energy, the horrible energy of national socialism, everything that he couldn't stand—bullying, exploitation, racism, hierarchy—was distilled, double distilled and distilled again into a system of cruelty and hatred, and Orwell felt the physical need to go and block its path with his own body in Spain. Being morally right about fascism is good enough, even if he was sometimes analytically wrong. And he was willing to fight and to kill and, much more important, the test of a revolutionary, to die in the struggle.

On communism, we know how clear-sighted he was in many ways. Though, I believe I might have to stand a challenge on this—I don't think that anyone has pointed out that in neither *Animal Farm* nor *Nineteen Eighty-Four* is there any [Vladimir] Lenin figure. There is only a [Leon] Trotsky and a Stalin. There's only [the characters of] Snowball and Napoleon [in *Animal Farm*]. There's only [the characters of] Goldstein and Big Brother [in *Nineteen Eighty-Four*]. The Lenin phase of the argument on the left about what went wrong with Marxism and with the revolution is by Orwell amazingly and interestingly and reprehensibly skipped. But he did see the point that remains with us, which is that any attempt to trade freedom for security contains a death trap within it. The one who can be persuaded or tries to persuade others that if you give up a little liberty you'll have a few more rations or a bit more protection runs the risk of losing both the freedom and the liberty *and* the security.

Orwell Overcame His Own Prejudices

And so when we are recalled to Orwellism and our memory of him by hearing ugly, euphemistic phrases, pretty names for nasty things such as "collateral damage," we should also bear in mind far more seductive phrases such as "homeland security," or the idea of security at all, or the idea of a homeland. All of these things need to be scrutinized and not just accepted. So Orwell's struggle with himself is extremely worth studying. His realization of his own contradictions and negations is part of the honor that I think is due to him.

And it is the same with the idea of the personal and the political. He wrestled massively with his prejudice against Jewish people and overcame it and wrote material on the roots and nature of anti-Semitism that could not have been written by someone who had never been a sufferer and that will stand as an extraordinarily clever and insightful and mordant critique of the most vulgar and most sinister mother of all prejudices. He may have had a distorted relationship with womanhood, but he married two very intelligent, tough-minded, independent, and highly educated women: Eileen O'Shaugnessy and Sonia Brownell.... Orwell got over his fear of the masses. He ceased to despise the working class in his country or the peasantry of others, perhaps even overcompensating, if anything, and being too sure of the wisdom of the people. Do misogynists like women too much or too little? It is not a question that I can resolve here but it is a question that might be decently asked. Overcompensating in the other direction is what has to be suspect about my original subject—the liberal softness on totalitarianism. Orwell was clever about patriotism. He knew enough to know that he suspected it and that it was suspect. But he also knew that it is an indispensable part of the human makeup. His argument was the following: You may think you've given up your own patriotism and have nothing but contempt for your own country. That doesn't mean you've given up patriotism altogether. So basic is this identification that it will be transferred to something else. You will begin to admire other people, other states, other communities for their solidarity, for their unity, for their brave leadership, for their marital qualities. This will be transferred into a vicarious admiration for others. As indeed it was by the intellectuals of the day into either fascism or communism. They only despise the martial and patriotic qualities of their own societies, but they couldn't destroy the instinct toward patriotism in themselves....

A thing that I am no longer interested in is the question of whether or not George Orwell would take my view or anyone else's if he was still with us. In 1984, it was actually possible that Orwell could have lived that long. We are now at the point that we are as far from him as he was from Dickens. We have to say goodbye to him as a contemporary and ask why it is, therefore, that he remains so vivid and actual in our own lives. My feeling is this and only this. Suppose it were possible to have this conversation. Suppose one could find out what he thought and more importantly, how he thought about any matter. All I can say for sure is that it would be a pleasure to disagree with him. And that is not a compliment I find one can very often bestow these days.

Social Issues in Literature

CHAPTER 2

George Orwell's *Nineteen Eighty-Four* and the Abuse of Power

Nineteen Eighty-Four
Is Terrifying Because
It Rings True

Irving Howe

American literary and social critic Irving Howe was an educator, author, and founder and editor of the journal Dissent. *A democratic socialist, he is the author of* Socialism and America.

Nineteen Eighty-Four *is George Orwell's nightmare vision of life in a totalitarian state. In the following selection, Irving Howe asserts that Orwell succeeds in capturing brilliantly—and terrifyingly—the essence of totalitarianism. Orwell defines totalitarianism by all the things it is lacking—emotion, spontaneity, liberties, personality, sexual passion, and human values, Howe maintains.*

Though not nearly so great a book [as Franz Kafka's *The Trial*], *1984* is in some ways more terrible. For it is not a paradigm and hardly a puzzle; whatever enigmas it raises concern not the imagination of the author but the life of our time. It does not take us away from, or beyond, our obsession with immediate social reality, and in reading the book we tend to say—the linguistic clumsiness conceals a deep truth—that the world of *1984* is "more real" than our own. The book appalls us because its terror, far from being inherent in the "human condition," is particular to our century; what haunts us is the sickening awareness that in *1984* Orwell has seized upon those elements of our public life that, given courage and intelligence, were avoidable.

A Book of Our Times

How remarkable a book *1984* really is, can be discovered only after a second reading. It offers true testimony, it speaks for our time. And because it derives from a perception of how our time may end, the book trembles with an eschatological fury that is certain to create among its readers, even those who sincerely believe they admire it, the most powerful kinds of resistance. It already has. Openly in England, more cautiously in America, there has arisen a desire among intellectuals to belittle Orwell's achievement, often in the guise of celebrating his humanity and his "goodness." They feel embarrassed before the apocalyptic desperation of the book, they begin to wonder whether it may not be just a little overdrawn and humorless, they even suspect it is tinged with the hysteria of the death-bed. Nor can it be denied that all of us would feel more comfortable if the book could be cast out. It is a remarkable book.

Whether it is a remarkable novel or a novel at all, seems unimportant. It is not, I suppose, really a novel, or at least it does not satisfy those expectations we have come to have with regard to the novel—expectations that are mainly the heritage of nineteenth century romanticism with its stress upon individual consciousness, psychological analysis and the study of intimate relations. One American critic, a serious critic, reviewed the book under the heading, "Truth Maybe, Not Fiction," as if thereby to demonstrate the strictness with which he held to distinctions of literary genre. Actually, he was demonstrating a certain narrowness of modern taste, for such a response to *1984* is possible only when discriminations are no longer made between fiction and the novel, which is but one kind of fiction, though the kind modern readers care for most.

A cultivated eighteenth century reader would never have said of *1984* that it may be true but isn't fiction, for it was then understood that fiction, like poetry, can have many modes and be open to many mixtures; the novel had not yet established its popular tyranny. What is more, the style of *1984*, which many readers take to be drab and uninspired or "sweaty," would have been appreciated by someone like [Daniel] Defoe, since Defoe would have immediately understood how the pressures of Orwell's subject, like the pressures of his own, demand a gritty and hammering factuality. The style of *1984* is the style of a man whose commitment to a dreadful vision is at war with the nausea to which that vision reduces him. So acute is this conflict that delicacies of phrasing or displays of rhetoric come to seem frivolous—*he has no time, he must get it all down.* Those who fail to see this, I am convinced, have succumbed to the pleasant tyrannies of estheticism; they have allowed their fondness for a cultivated style to blind them to the urgencies of prophetic expression. The last thing Orwell cared about when he wrote *1984*, the last thing he should have cared about, was literature.

Individuality Destroyed in *1984*

Another complaint one often hears is that there are no credible or "three-dimensional" characters in the book. Apart from its rather facile identification of credibility with a particular treatment of character, the complaint involves a failure to see that in some books an extended amount of psychological specification or even dramatic incident can be disastrous. In *1984* Orwell is trying to present the kind of world in which individuality has become obsolete and personality a crime. The whole idea of the self as something precious and inviolable is a *cultural* idea, and as we understand it, a product of the liberal era; but Orwell has imagined a world in which the self, whatever subterranean existence it manages to eke out, is no longer a significant value, not even a value to be violated.

Winston Smith and Julia come through as rudimentary figures because they are slowly learning, and at great peril to themselves, what it means to be human. Their experiment in the rediscovery of the human, which is primarily an experiment in the possibilities of solitude, leads them to cherish two things that are fundamentally hostile to the totalitarian outlook: a life of contemplativeness and the joy of "purposeless"—that is, free—sexual passion. But this experiment cannot go very far, as they themselves know; it is inevitable that they be caught and destroyed.

Partly, that is the meaning and the pathos of the book. Were it possible, in the world of 1984, to show human character in anything resembling genuine freedom, in its play of spontaneous desire and caprice—it would not be the world of 1984. So that in a slightly obtuse way the complaint that Orwell's characters seem thin testifies to the strength of the book, for it is a complaint directed not against his technique but against his primary assumptions.

The book cannot be understood, nor can it be properly valued, simply by resorting to the usual literary categories, for it posits a situation in which these categories are no longer significant. Everything has hardened into politics, the leviathan has swallowed man. About such a world it is, strictly speaking, impossible to write a novel, if only because the human relationships taken for granted in the novel are here suppressed. The book must first be approached through politics, yet not as a political study or treatise. It is something else, at once a model and a vision—a model of the totalitarian state in its "pure" or "essential" form and a vision of what this state can do to human life. Yet the theme of the conflict between ideology and emotion, as at times their fusion and mutual reinforcement, . . . is still to be found in *1984*, as a dim underground motif. Without this theme, there could be no dramatic conflict in a work of fiction dominated by politics. Winston Smith's effort to reconstruct the old tune about the bells of St. Clement is a token of his desire to regain the condition of humanness, which is here nothing more than a capacity for so "useless" a feeling as nostalgia. Between the tune and Oceania there can be no peace.

1984 projects a nightmare in which politics has displaced humanity and the state has stifled society. In a sense, it is a profoundly antipolitical book, full of hatred for the kind of world in which public claims destroy the possibilities for private life; and this conservative side of Orwell's outlook he suggests, perhaps unconsciously, through the first name of his hero. But if the image of [Winston] Churchill is thus raised in order to celebrate, a little wryly, the memory of the bad (or as Winston Smith comes to feel, the good) old days, the opposing image of [Leon] Trotsky is raised, a little skeptically, in order to discover the inner meanings of totalitarian society. When Winston Smith learns to think of Oceania as a *problem*—which is itself to commit a "crimethink"—he turns to the forbidden work of Emmanuel Goldstein, *The Theory and Practice of Oligarchical Collectivism*, clearly a replica of Trotsky's *The Revolution Betrayed*. The power and intelligence of *1984* partly derives from a tension between these images; even as Orwell understood the need for politics in the modern world, he felt a profound distaste for the ways of political life, and he was honest enough not to try to suppress one or another side of this struggle within himself.

1984 Evokes the Tone of Totalitarianism

No other book has succeeded so completely in rendering the essential quality of totalitarianism. *1984* is limited in scope; it does not pretend to investigate the genesis of the totalitarian state, nor the laws of its economy, nor the prospect for its survival; it simply evokes the "tone" of life in a totalitarian society. And since it is not a realistic novel, it can treat Oceania as an *extreme instance*, one that might never actually exist but which illuminates the nature of societies that do exist.

Orwell's profoundest insight is that in a totalitarian world man's life is shorn of dynamic possibilities. The end of life is completely predictable in its beginning, the beginning merely a manipulated preparation for the end. There is no opening for surprise, for that spontaneous animation which is the to-ken of and justification for freedom. Oceanic society may evolve through certain stages of economic development, but the life of its members is static, a given and measured quan-tity that can neither rise to tragedy nor tumble to comedy. Human personality, as we have come to grasp for it in a class society and hope for it in a classless society, is obliterated; man becomes a function of a process he is never allowed to understand or control. The fetishism of the state replaces the fetishism of commodities. . . .

Sexual Impulses Weakened

At only a few points can one question Orwell's vision of to-talitarianism, and even these involve highly problematic mat-ters. If they are errors at all, it is only to the extent that they drive valid observations too hard: Orwell's totalitarian society is at times more *total* than we can presently imagine.

One such problem has to do with the relation between the state and "human nature." Granted that human nature is itself a cultural concept with a history of change behind it; granted that the pressures of fear and force can produce extreme varia-tions in human conduct. There yet remains the question: to what extent can a terrorist regime suppress or radically alter the fundamental impulses of man? Is there a constant in hu-man nature which no amount of terror or propaganda can destroy?

In Oceania the sexual impulse, while not destroyed, has been remarkably weakened among the members of the Outer Party. For the faithful, sexual energy is transformed into po-litical hysteria. There is a harrowing passage in which Smith remembers his sexual relations with his former wife, a loyal party member who would submit herself once a week, as if for an ordeal and resisting even while insisting, in order to procreate for the party. The only thing she did not feel was pleasure. . . .

That Orwell has here come upon an important tendency in modern life, that the totalitarian state is inherently an enemy of erotic freedom, seems to me indisputable. And we know from the past that the sexual impulse can be heavily suppressed. In Puritan communities, for example, sex was regarded with great suspicion, and it is not hard to imagine that even in marriage the act of love might bring the Puritans very little pleasure. But it should be remembered that in Puritan communities hostility toward sex was interwoven with a powerful faith: men mortified themselves in behalf of God. By contrast, Oceania looks upon faith not merely as suspect but downright dangerous, for its rulers prefer mechanical assent to intellectual fervor or zealous belief. (They have probably read enough history to know that in the Protestant era enthusiasm had a way of turning into individualism.)

Given these circumstances, is it plausible that the Outer Party members would be able to discard erotic pleasure so completely? Is this not cutting too close to the limit of indestructible human needs? I should think that in a society so pervaded by boredom and grayness as Oceania is, there would be a pressing hunger for erotic adventure, to say nothing of experiments in perversion.

A totalitarian society can force people to do many things that violate their social and physical desires; it may even teach them to receive pain with quiet resignation; but I doubt that it can break down the fundamental, if sometimes ambiguous, distinction between pleasure and pain. Man's biological make-up requires him to obtain food, and, with less regularity or insistence, sex; and while society can do a great deal—it has—to dim the pleasures of sex and reduce the desire for food, it seems reasonable to assume that even when consciousness has been blitzed, the "animal drives" of man cannot be violated as thoroughly as Orwell suggests. In the long run, these drives may prove to be one of the most enduring forces of resistance to the totalitarian state.

Does not Orwell imply something of the sort when he shows Winston Smith turning to individual reflection and Julia to private pleasure? What is the source of their rebellion if not the "innate" resistance of their minds and bodies to the destructive pressures of Oceania? It is clear that they are no more intelligent or sensitive—certainly no more heroic—than most Outer Party members. And if their needs as human beings force these two quite ordinary people to rebellion, may not the same thing happen to others? . . .

The Exercise of Power

Finally, there is Orwell's extremely interesting though questionable view of the dynamics of power in a totalitarian state. As he portrays the party oligarchy in Oceania, it is the first ruling class of modern times to dispense with ideology. It makes no claim to be ruling in behalf of humanity, the workers, the nation or anyone but itself; it rejects as naive the rationale of [Fyodor Dostoyevsky's] Grand Inquisitor that he oppresses the ignorant to accomplish their salvation. O'Brien, the representative of the Inner Party, says: "The Party seeks power entirely for its own sake. We are not interested in the good of the others; we are interested solely in power." The Stalinists and Nazis, he adds, had approached this view of power, but only in Oceania has all pretense to serving humanity—that is, all ideology—been discarded.

Social classes have at least one thing in common: an appetite for power. The bourgeoisie sought power, not primarily as an end in itself (whatever that vague phrase might mean), but in order to be free to expand its economic and social activity. The ruling class of the new totalitarian society, especially in Russia, is different, however, from previous ruling classes of our time: it does not think of political power as a means toward a non-political end, as to some extent the bourgeoisie did; it looks upon political power as its essential end. For in a society where there is no private property the distinction between economic and political power becomes invisible.

So far this would seem to bear out Orwell's view. But if the ruling class of the totalitarian state does not conceive of political power as primarily a channel to tangible economic privileges, what *does* political power mean to it?

At least in the West, no modern ruling class has yet been able to dispense with ideology. All have felt an overwhelming need to rationalize their power, to proclaim some admirable objective as a justification for detestable acts. Nor is this mere slyness or hypocrisy; the rulers of a modern society can hardly survive without a certain degree of sincere belief in their own claims. They cling to ideology not merely to win and hold followers, but to give themselves psychological and moral assurance.

Can one imagine a twentieth century ruling class capable of discarding these supports and acknowledging to itself the true nature of its motives? I doubt it. Many Russian bureaucrats, in the relaxation of private cynicism, may look upon their Marxist vocabulary as a useful sham; but they must still cling to some vague assumption that somehow their political conduct rests upon ultimate sanctions. Were this not so, the totalitarian ruling class would find it increasingly difficult, perhaps impossible, to sustain its morale. It would go soft, it would become corrupted in the obvious ways, it would lose the fanaticism that is essential to its survival.

But ideology aside, there remains the enigma of totalitarian power. And it *is* an enigma. Many writers have probed the origins of totalitarianism, the dynamics of its growth, the psychological basis of its appeal, the economic policies it employs when in power. But none of the theorists who study totalitarianism can tell us very much about the "ultimate purpose" of the Nazis or the Stalinists; in the end they come up against the same difficulties as does Winston Smith in *1984* when he says, "I understand HOW: I do not understand WHY."

Toward what end do the rulers of Oceania strive? They want power; they want to enjoy the sense of exercising their power, which means to test their ability to cause those below them to suffer. Yet the question remains, why do they kill millions of people, why do they find pleasure in torturing and humiliating people they know to be innocent? For that matter, why did the Nazis and Stalinists? What is the image of the world they desire, the vision by which they live?

I doubt that such questions can presently be answered, and it may be that they are not even genuine problems. A movement in which terror and irrationality play so great a role may finally have no goal beyond terror and irrationality; to search for an ultimate end that can be significantly related to its immediate activity may itself be a rationalist fallacy.

Orwell has been criticized by Isaac Deutscher for succumbing to a "mysticism of cruelty" in explaining the behavior of Oceania's rulers, which means, I suppose, that Orwell does not entirely accept any of the usual socio-economic theories about the aims of totalitarianism. It happens, however, that neither Mr. Deutscher nor anyone else has yet been able to provide a satisfactory explanation for that systematic excess in destroying human values which is a central trait of totalitarianism. I do not say that the mystery need remain with us forever, since it is possible that in time we shall be able to dissolve it into a series of problems more easily manageable. Meanwhile, however, it seems absurd to attack a writer for acknowledging with rare honesty his sense of helplessness before the "ultimate" meaning of totalitarianism—especially if that writer happens to have given us the most graphic vision of totalitarianism that has yet been composed. For with *1984* we come to the heart of the matter, the whiteness of the whiteness.

Even while noting these possible objections to Orwell's book, I have been uneasily aware that they might well be irrelevant—as irrelevant, say, as the objection that no one can be so small as [Jonathan] Swift's Lilliputians. What is more, it is extremely important to note that the world of 1984 is *not* totalitarianism as we know it, but totalitarianism after its world triumph. Strictly speaking, the society of Oceania might be called post-totalitarian. But I have let my objections stand simply because it may help the reader see Orwell's book somewhat more clearly if he considers their possible value and decides whether to accept or reject them. . . .

In later generations *1984* may have little more than "historic interest." If the world of 1984 does come to pass, no one will read it except perhaps the rulers who will reflect upon its extraordinary prescience. If the world of *1984* does not come to pass, people may well feel that this book was merely a symptom of private disturbance, a nightmare. But we know better: we know that the nightmare is ours.

Nineteen Eighty-Four Depicts the Irrationality of Totalitarianism

Alex Zwerdling

Alex Zwerdling is professor emeritus in English at the University of California, Berkeley, and the author of Virginia Woolf and the Real World.

In the following selection, Zwerdling argues that, although Nineteen Eighty-Four *is often linked with Aldous Huxley's* Brave New World, *it shares more in common with Yevgeny Zamyatin's* We. *Both novels present dystopias that are irrational. In the case of* Nineteen Eighty-Four, *Zwerdling asserts, the roots of George Orwell's vision are not only in Communist Russia, but also in the Nazi concentration camps.*

By the time he came to write *Nineteen Eighty-Four*, [Orwell] was conscious of an unprecedented irrational streak in modern politics that could not be understood in classic terms: economic first causes, class warfare, progress and reaction, international competition, *Realpolitik* [politics based on real life] and all the other rational explanations of what went on in public life. By comparison, his earlier political allegory, *Animal Farm*, was built on a more familiar foundation: class distinctions, the permanence of privilege, the predictable stages of a revolution, and so on. Perhaps it was the intellectual conservatism of the book's conceptual framework that allowed Orwell to write such a spare, elegant, perfectly controlled parable. All the forces in *Animal Farm*, including that of the author's vision, are essentially rational.

Orwell Saw Politics as Irrational

Only a few years later, such a foundation would no longer strike him as sound. He had come to feel that political explanations would have to use the vocabulary of mental illness, religious zealotry, and primal emotions. "We shall get nowhere," he wrote in 1946, "unless we start by recognising that political behaviour is largely non-rational, that the world is suffering from some kind of mental disease which must be diagnosed before it can be cured." The writers who interested him most had grasped this essential point. His model for the world of the future was not to be the utopias of [H.G.] Wells or [Aldous] Huxley but the darker vision embodied in [Yevgeny] Zamyatin's *We*. For "Wells is too sane to understand the modern world"; and Huxley also suffers in the comparison: "It is this intuitive grasp of the irrational side of totalitarianism—human sacrifice, cruelty as an end in itself, the worship of a Leader who is credited with divine attributes—that makes Zamyatin's book superior to Huxley's." Orwell's most sustained attempt to analyze this vision of modern political life is the essay "Notes on Nationalism," written in 1945 as he was thinking out his last novel. It consistently uses the descriptive terminology of mental illness: *obsession, fixation, schizophrenia* are all words applied to modern political behavior. Politics has become a realm in which free-floating fantasy and urgent emotion are in control—"fear, hatred, jealousy and power worship are involved," he writes, and as a result "the sense of reality becomes unhinged."

This sense of a subterranean, deeply irrational current in public affairs is part of Orwell's legacy. . . .

The Roots of *Nineteen Eighty-Four* Are in Concentration Camps

Nineteen Eighty-Four attempts to evoke this realm of perverse, malignant fantasy. Its historical roots seem to me to lie as much in the first postwar descriptions of what went on in the concentration camps as in the earlier reports of the Soviet purges, though of course the two are related. But the seedtime of Orwell's novel—the mid-1940s in which he was planning the book and composing the first draft—coincided with the first widespread publicity about just what had happened in Dachau and Buchenwald, in Belsen and Treblinka and Auschwitz [Nazi concentration and death camps]. Those names were carved in the Western memory as one camp after another was liberated by the Allied armies in 1945. The spring 1945 volume of *The Official Index to The Times* (London) had a new subheading under Germany: "atrocities." The list of relevant pieces in the *Times* for this three-month period alone fills four columns. . . .

These journalistic descriptions were followed in the next two or three years by many important book-length studies, including those written by [Holocaust] survivors like David Rousset. It is clear that Orwell was deeply interested in such works, that he read many of them, and that he took the camps to be symptomatic of the pervasive irrationalism of modern political life. As he writes to Rousset's English translator, "The point is that these forced-labour camps are part of the pattern of our time, & are a very interesting though horrible phenomenon." They illustrated better than any other fact of contemporary history that the images of nightmare—of monstrously powerful opponents, helpless victims incomprehensibly assaulted, prisons without doors, purposeless torture, sadomasochistic pain and pleasure—were more useful to an understanding of what was going on in the real world than the ordinary waking observation of "normal men."

A Dream World

This is why dreams and fantasies are so pervasive in *Nineteen Eighty-Four*. The boundary between reality and imagination is consistently blurred in the novel, and we are often left uncertain about whether something actually happened. A voice murmurs, "Don't worry, Winston: you are in my keeping. For seven years I have watched over you. Now the turning-point has come. I shall save you, I shall make you perfect." But Winston cannot remember if the voice is O'Brien's or whether he heard it "in drugged sleep, or in normal sleep, or even in a moment of wakefulness." Winston's dreams are recurrent and always revelatory. The dream of the voice that tells him "We shall meet in the place where there is no darkness," of his mother in a sinking ship cradling his baby sister, the recurrent dream of the "Golden Country" and that of "standing in front of a wall of darkness," on the other side of which "there was something unendurable, something too dreadful to be faced": all are significant and illuminate his actual situation and experience. Orwell consistently emphasizes the vital importance of these unwilled excursions into fantasy, and he draws attention to the links between them and reality: "It was one of those dreams which, while retaining the characteristic dream scenery, are a continuation of one's intellectual life, and in which one becomes aware of facts and ideas which still seem new and valuable after one is awake."

Nineteen Eighty-Four also uses the world of childhood fantasy to stretch the limits of "normal" adult consciousness and tap the world of the irrational. The seemingly innocent nursery rhyme that begins "Oranges and lemons, say the bells of St. Clement's" is gradually recalled in the course of the book: O'Brien himself ominously provides the last line. And when Winston and Julia are arrested, the voice of the "friendly" antique dealer, Mr. Charrington, who had recited for Winston the rhymes "about four and twenty blackbirds, and another about a cow with a crumpled horn, and another about the death of poor Cock Robin," now mocks him with a final message from the nursery: "Here comes a candle to light you to bed, here comes a chopper to chop off your head!" The anarchic, incomprehensible violence of childhood fantasy meshed all too easily with the bizarre and frightening reality of the modern police state. . . .

The State Becomes a Tyrannical Parent

[Orwell and other analysts of totalitarianism have] argued that such regimes deliberately set out to reduce the competent, independent adult to a state of childish helplessness and fear. [Social scientist] Bruno Bettelheim's important book on the concentration camps, *The Informed Heart*, offers the best description of this sinister process. His whole section on "Childlike Behavior" emphasizes the analogy between prisoner and helpless child. He concludes, "There seems no doubt that the tasks they [the prisoners] were given, as well as the mistreatment they had to endure, contributed to the disintegration of their self respect and made it impossible to see themselves and each other as fully adult persons any more."

Bettelheim goes on to apply this theory to the ordinary subjects of totalitarian regimes outside the concentration camps. "Only in infancy did other persons, our parents, have the power to throw us into desperate inner turmoil if our wishes conflicted with theirs.... This power for creating unmanageable inner conflicts in the child must be compared with the power of the total state to create similar conflicts in the minds of its subjects."

Totalitarian regimes adopted a deliberate policy of infantilizing their citizens as a way of giving the ruler uncontested power over their lives.

The politics of such regimes were the politics of family life. This analogy is at the heart of *Nineteen Eighty-Four*. Orwell describes a world in which familial loyalty is deliberately undermined so that the displaced emotions can be appropriated by the state. The solidarity of the family is treated as a threat to party loyalty and is therefore systematically weakened. Children are encouraged to betray their parents. They are organized into single-generation, transfamilial groups (the Spies; the Youth League). Constant obligatory adult activities at the Community Centre take up evenings and weekends that might otherwise have been spent with the family. Marriages are subject to Party approval and prevented if the partners betray too much affection. Sex is discouraged except as a means of procreation. The home is not a sanctuary but a goldfish bowl.

In *Nineteen Eighty-Four*, the regime strives to become the heir of the moribund family and systematically appropriates the emotional capital of that institution. Its leader, Big Brother, combines the qualities of disciplinarian father and loyal sibling. Even the invented conspiracy against him is called "the Brotherhood." What Winston Smith at first misses from this world is the sense of maternal protection. He dreams ceaselessly about his mother: "His mother's memory tore at his heart because she had died loving him, when he was too young and selfish to love her in return, and because somehow, he did not remember how, she had sacrificed herself to a conception of loyalty that was private and unalterable." Her love was unconditional and uncoercive, and there are really no substitutes for such affection in the public world Winston inhabits.

His task is to transform this need for maternal sponsorship into one of the emotions licensed by the state. The pressure for him to do just this is relentless, and eventually he succumbs. His disturbing response to O'Brien's torture is a stage in this process: "For a moment he clung to O'Brien like a baby, curiously comforted by the heavy arm round his shoulders." There are only two characters in the novel who address Winston by his first name—his mother, and O'Brien. Others refer to him as "comrade" or "Smith"; Julia calls him "dear" or "love" but never uses his name; the voice on the telescreen barks "6079 Smith W." Only O'Brien persistently uses the intimate, familiar, endearing form of address associated with childhood. It is not entirely ironic that the building in which Winston Smith is being tortured is called the Ministry of Love. By the last paragraph of the novel, when all his other bonds—including the loving bond to Julia—have been cut, he finally twists the strands of his need for mother, father, sibling, and lover into a single emotion.

> O stubborn, self-willed exile from the loving breast! Two gin-scented tears trickled down the sides of his nose. But it was all right, everything was all right, the struggle was finished. He had won the victory over himself. He loved Big Brother.

The emotions recorded in such passages echo the feelings described in the psychoanalytic literature on sadomasochism and reopen the question of whether Orwell's vision of totalitarianism is not fundamentally skewed by some neurotic aberration. . . .

The Burden of Freedom

In social psychology, the individual psyche becomes a microcosm of society itself and a way of studying public life at the cellular level. The kinds of questions that social psychologists try to answer are attempts to explain sociopolitical behavior by linking it to fundamental human needs and fears. "Can freedom become a burden, too heavy for man to bear, something he tries to escape from?" Erich Fromm asks. "Is there not also, perhaps, besides an innate desire for freedom, an instinctive wish for submission? . . . Is there a hidden satisfaction in submitting, and what is its essence? What is it that creates in men an insatiable lust for power?"

Any reader of *Nineteen Eighty-Four* will recognize these questions. Orwell was a writer of fiction, not a social psychologist. But his deep interest in totalitarianism led him to think about issues of freedom and submission, power and impotence in similar terms. Winston Smith has many of the characteristics described in some of the works of social psychology written in the decade that produced Orwell's novel. He is of course a rebel on the surface and thinks he is joining a conspiracy to bring down a despotic regime. But Orwell

In this scene from BBC TV's production of 1984, O'Brien (played by Joseph O'Connor) tortures Winston Smith (played by David Buck). Orwell's novel presents the irrationality of totalitarianism. Larry Ellis/express/Hulton Archive/Getty Images.

makes it clear that at a deeper level Winston wills his own degradation because of his wish to submit. He knows he will be caught, has no chance of escape, yet deliberately chooses a path that can only lead him to a place where he will be—in his own words—"utterly without power of any kind." And when O'Brien stands revealed not as a fellow conspirator but as an agent of the regime, he says to Winston in words that ring true, "You knew this. . . . Don't deceive yourself. You did know it—you have always known it."

O'Brien is the instrument of Winston's reformation, the force that will allow him to shed his painful, undesired isolation, the confessor who will understand and save him from himself. Winston reflects that "at bottom it did not matter whether O'Brien was a friend or an enemy. . . . O'Brien was a person who could be talked to. Perhaps one did not want to be loved so much as to be understood. . . . In some sense that went deeper than friendship, they were intimates." This is why he freely surrenders his last secret, the core of his resistance to the state. When O'Brien asks him "Can you think of a single degradation that has not happened to you?" Winston helpfully answers. "I have not betrayed Julia." He thus initiates the final torture with the cage of rats in which he surrenders that last, rival loyalty. "Do it to Julia! Do it to Julia!" he screams. "Not me! Julia!"

Orwell's novel depicts a world in which societal pressure has become so relentless that the isolated individual no longer even wishes to hold out against it. The psychic price is too high. Orwell understood the emotional appeal of [Adolf] Hitler's slogan, "Better an end with horror than a horror without end." In *Nineteen Eighty-Four* he imagined his way into the mind and heart of an unheroic character whose sense of isolation has become unbearable enough to make him want to get rid of the independent self that is creating it. The forces that can lead to such a surrender are analyzed in Bettelheim's *The Informed Heart*.

The more absolute the tyranny, the more debilitated the subject, the more tempting to him to "regain" strength by becoming part of the tyranny and thus enjoy its power. In accepting all this one can attain, or reattain; some inner integration through conformity. But the price one must pay is to identify with the tyranny without reservation, in brief, to give up autonomy.

This, one might say, is what happens at the end of *Nineteen Eighty-Four*. Winston's final, agonized surrender is his attempt to follow O'Brien's prescription and promise of relief. If only he will submit completely and merge his will in that of the Party, the intolerable burden of his independence will be lifted.

All this may help us to understand the psychology of the victim, of the follower. But what can account for the actions of the leader, of the victimizer? The two questions interested Orwell equally, and he did his best to grasp what he called "the special quality in modern life that makes a major human motive out of the impulse to bully others." . . .

Victim and Victimizer Are Linked

[Orwell] was not by temperament a propagandistic or melodramatic writer: quite the opposite. The absolute distinction between victim and victimizer that the times demanded struck him as an unacceptable simplification. Though *Nineteen Eighty-Four* has its melodramatic moments, it also regularly challenges the neat categories of that genre. Julia is not an idealistic rebel but a hedonist intent on her own pleasure and largely indifferent to others. Winston Smith betrays her, he is not cast in the heroic mold, and some of his reactions suggest that he is capable of committing his own "atrocities." As he looks at the "silly blond face" of a foolish colleague who unintentionally prevents him from talking to Julia, he "had a hallucination of himself smashing a pick-axe right into the middle of it." And he readily agrees "to throw sulphuric acid in a child face" if it would serve the interests of the revolutionary

Brotherhood. The connections between these impulses and O'Brien's vision of the future—"a boot stamping on a human face—for ever"—are obvious. And O'Brien is far from being a stock villain. He is (if his speeches can be trusted) a fanatical idealist, a true believer. His is also incomparably the most powerful intelligence in the book, as Winston repeatedly feels: "There was no idea that he had ever had, or could have, that O'Brien had not long ago known, examined, and rejected. His mind *contained* Winston's mind."

All these passages reveal that victim and victimizer inhabit a common mental landscape. This insight, like so many others in Orwell's work, finds echoes both in the early psychoanalytic studies and in the contemporary analyses of totalitarianism. The psychological predisposition involved, after all, is called sadomasochism. The term itself insists on linking the roles of victim and victimizer and indeed of treating them as inter-changeable—different parts played on different occasions, as great actors have sometimes alternated the roles of Othello and Iago in successive performances [of Shakespeare's *Othello*]. Freud claimed that it was impossible to decide "whether the pleasure attaching to the beating-phantasy was to be de-scribed as sadistic or masochistic." Otto Fenichel's *Psychoanalytic Theory of Neurosis* describes the sadomasochist in a passage that illuminates Winston's cry "Do it to Julia!" "If a person is able to do to others what he fears may be done to him, he no longer has to be afraid. . . . What might happen to the subject passively is done actively by him, in anticipation of attack, to others." And Fromm saw the bond between victim and aggressor as fundamentally symbiotic, a state of mutual dependence between persons cut from the same cloth. "People are not sadistic *or* masochistic, but there is a constant oscillation between the active and the passive side of the symbiotic complex, so that it is often difficult to determine which side of it is operating at a given moment." . . .

Nineteen Eighty-Four Is About Orwell's Day

Despite his deep affection for England. Orwell disliked [its] mood of national self-congratulation. It ignored Britain's tragic experience in its own empire—in Ireland, in India, in South Africa (where concentration camps were first used during the Boer War). And it created a hopeless impediment to grasping issues of great importance. He was convinced that to understand the darker side of modern politics one could not make simple distinctions between "them" and "us." So he [writes], for instance, that "the starting point for any investigation of antisemitism should not be 'Why does this obviously irrational belief appeal to other people?' but 'Why does antisemitism appeal to *me?* What is there about it that I feel to be true?' . . . In that way one might get some clues that would lead to its psychological roots."

The fear of the reader's incredulity, indifference, and complacency all helped to give *Nineteen Eighty-Four* its particular form and texture. He told his publisher in 1947 that this "novel about the future" was proving exceptionally difficult to write because "it is in a sense a fantasy, but in the form of a naturalistic novel." The imaginative excursions in the book— essential as we have seen them to be—were kept in check by a more pervasive circumstantiality of detail, an almost photographic realism. The decaying block of flats where Winston lives, with its smell of boiled cabbage, its lift that seldom works, its blocked drainpipes: the seedy antique shop in a slum quarter where he and Julia find temporary shelter; the Sunday outing to the country that begins at Paddington Station—all would have struck a British reader of the 1940s as the familiar scenery of his own world. . . .

The same logic demanded that the story be set in England, and in a time that most readers in 1949 could easily imagine as part of their own lives—not in Utopia or in Erewhon, not in some science fiction future that bore no resemblance to the present day. It also dictated that his hero should have a quintessentially English name. All these choices were determined by Orwell's fear that readers would dismiss his imagined future as something having to do with "them," not with "us." For this reason too his protagonist is a kind of everyman. He matters because he might be any one of us if we had the misfortune to find ourselves in his situation. He is not idealized but neither is he perverse. The disturbing violence of his fantasy life, his rapid shifts between resistance and cowardice, his final breakdown are all consequences of the irrational political world in which he finds himself, and which has its roots in the possible, the actual, though it speaks the language of bad dreams. It would be reassuring to think that the world Orwell created in his fiction really *was* only the product of his paranoid imagination. But by this point in the century in which he and we grew up we know that it was not.

His reconceptualization of political life may well prove to be the most enduring aspect of *Nineteen Eighty-Four*. The year itself will come and go. As a piece of prophecy Orwell's novel is not remarkable for its detailed accuracy. Its predictions have more the flavor of 1948 than 1984. But the core of the vision is not really dated, because Orwell's understanding of irrational politics seems increasingly persuasive. Terrorism, fanatical dedication to a cause, religious wars, resurgent nationalisms, political incarceration and torture, the manipulation of public response through fraud, the spreading network of surveillance: who would not instantly recognize these characteristics of the political world of our time? There is of course an important countertradition in democratic countries that might be called rational politics. Our duly elected representatives enact legislation. Guilt and innocence are determined in courts of law. Our leaders make promises, negotiate treaties, try to persuade us of the value of their programs. But though these public events are often taken seriously and are not unreal, the sense of them as masking more anarchic impulses has grown. There is an increasing cynicism—by this time widely felt—about political appearances and a shared sense that what really matters goes on behind the scenes or beyond the confines of normal political life and is largely beyond our control. The vision is not attractive. Orwell was one of the first writers with the courage to face it and the talent to give it unforgettable fictional life. He produced a fantasy in the shape of a naturalistic novel. The naturalism was on the surface, the fantasy at the core. But the fantasy was a nightmare, and the nightmare was the history of his time from which—like [James] Joyce's Stephen Dedalus [character in *Ulysses*]—he was trying in vain to awake.

Nineteen Eighty-Four Predicts the Downfall of Totalitarianism by the Working Class

Richard J. Voorhees

Richard J. Voorhees, author of The Paradox of George Orwell, *was an English professor at Purdue University from 1946 to 1982.*

Critics who interpret Nineteen Eighty-Four *as a prediction of the triumph of totalitarianism are wrong, according to Richard J. Voorhees in the following essay. George Orwell intended his novel not as a prophecy but as a warning of what could happen. Voorhees asserts that a closer reading of* Nineteen Eighty-Four *shows that it is those in the working class, the proles, who have retained their humanity throughout the book; these are the people that Orwell believes will rebuild a better society, Voorhees maintains.*

An American edition of George Orwell's *Keep the Aspidistra Flying* was published early this year [1956]. It was a long time in coming (the English edition appeared in 1936), but it would not have come at all had not two other books by Orwell been extremely successful. Until four years before he died he was almost unknown in this country. In 1946 and 1949, however, *Animal Farm* and *Nineteen Eighty-Four* were best sellers. They have continued to sell, and by now Orwell must be better known in America than all but two or three other British writers of the past ten years. But he is not so much read as misread. The common reader sees *Nineteen Eighty-*

Richard J. Voorhees, "*Nineteen Eighty-Four*: No Failure of Nerve," *College English*, vol. 18, no. 2, November 1956, pp. 101–102.

Four as a prediction of universal totalitarianism in the near future. Critics make matters worse by suggesting that Orwell could not face the world he foresaw and so took tuberculosis as a way out. In the following paragraphs I shall try to show that Orwell, who in the first place was a very brave man and in the second place was always suspicious of political prediction, did not turn coward and prophet of doom the year before he died.

Propaganda, Not Prophecy

To be sure, the world of *Nineteen Eighty-Four* seems, if not altogether hopeless, at least altogether horrible: a world ruled by men whose ends are unlimited power and whose means are unlimited violence. The cult of power and the use of violence are, indeed, major themes of Orwell's writing during the last fourteen years of his life. But they did not frighten him to death. He hated men who were power-hungry, but he despised men who bowed down to power. He kept harping on totalitarianism because he believed that people in democratic countries needed to be constantly reminded of it. In *Nineteen Eighty-Four* he was writing his fiercest piece of propaganda; he seems to have felt about it as G.K. Chesterton felt about Allied propaganda in World War I: "The case against horror should be horrible."

Orwell also shared Chesterton's enthusiasm for the past. Of course, he was not a medievalist, but he was a Dickensian. In much of his work [Charles] Dickens himself was, as a matter of fact, writing about a world which was already ceasing to exist, providing a record of the way that an earlier generation had lived. In *Coming Up for Air* Orwell does exactly the same thing. One of the worst features of the world of *Nineteen Eighty-Four* is that there are no such records anywhere, and one of Winston Smith's most frustrating experiences is his failure to find out what society was like fifty years before his time. Yet Winston has some fragmentary memories which tell him that life was once better. He also has a sort of ancestral memory by which he visits in his dreams what he calls "the Golden Country."

Now the interesting thing about "the Golden Country" is that it is precisely the sort of place that George Bowling, the hero of *Coming Up for Air*, remembers from his boyhood. But not only the worlds that Winston Smith and George Bowling remember, but also those in which they actually live are remarkably alike. Descriptive passages could be switched back and forth between the earlier book, which is set in the period just before World War II, and the later. This correspondence is one indication that *Nineteen Eighty-Four* is not intended as prophecy. A more explicit indication that Orwell is not going into the crystal-gazing business is the Appendix of the book, entitled "The Principles of Newspeak." "Even in the early decades of the twentieth century," Orwell writes, "telescoped words and phrases had been ... characteristic ... of political language, and it had been noticed that the tendency to use abbreviations of this kind was most marked in totalitarian countries. Examples were such words as Nazi, Gestapo, Comintern. . . ." The purpose of telescoping words and phrases is to squeeze their original meanings out of them, so that, in the strictest sense of the expression, people will not know what they are talking about. What Orwell does in *Nineteen Eighty-Four* is to carry the telescoping process to its logical conclusion. A friend of Winston's who is working on the eleventh and supposedly definitive edition of the *Newspeak Dictionary* explains that the purpose of his work is not to add words to the language, but to subtract them from it, to reduce the range of thinking so that unorthodox thoughts will simply be impossible. Orwell's point, however, is not that a perfect version of totalitarian language will someday be created, but that workable versions have already been created. The danger lies, as it were, not in the eleventh edition of the *Dictionary*, but in the tenth. In his earlier essay on the same theme, "Politics and the English Language," Orwell does not exaggerate the trend of totalitarian linguistics; in *Nineteen Eighty-Four* he does, and readers have mistaken caricature for prophecy.

The Downfall of Totalitarianism

For the most part, however, Orwell took totalitarianism just about as he found it. There is nothing novel in damming up the sexual instinct and canalizing it into leader-worship, hatred, and war hysteria. Neither is there anything original in distorting the normal feelings of the family to political ends, so that the child becomes an extension of the secret police, spying on his frightened parents day and night. As for the police themselves, the constant surveillance of citizens, the technique of arrests, the inquisatorial routine—all these things are recognizable even to people who during the past twenty-five years have got their political education from the movies. And those who read only the headlines of the newspapers are familiar with the sudden switching of enemies, the doctrine that the end justifies the means, the five-year plans [of the Soviet Union], the claim to have invented everything.

Naturally, Orwell has not described the conditions of totalitarianism just for the intellectual exercise. His book is a warning. But it is no more an indication of what the future must be like than a danger sign on a highway is an indication of an inevitable wreck. Read literally, of course, it predicts the rise of totalitarian governments to power over the entire world. But read literally, it also predicts their downfall. It is time that some notice be taken of the tenses and moods of the verbs in the Appendix: "Newspeak was the official language of Oceania. . . ." "It was expected that Newspeak would have finally superseded Oldspeak . . . by about the year 2050." Read in the light of Goldstein's writings, even the torture scenes convey an intimation that the Party will not be in power forever. In Goldstein's book Winston learns that a class falls from power when it becomes stupid or loses heart. O'Brien,

Winston's torturer, is not stupid, but for one moment his behavior suggests that the Party may lose heart, that there are flaws in the pattern of ruthless ambition. At that moment O'Brien looks at Winston "gravely and rather sadly." O'Brien is not Arthur Koestler's Rubashov or Ivanov, but neither is he Koestler's Gletkin [in *Darkness at Noon*].

The chief hope for Winston Smith's world, however, is not in the O'Briens, who have remained human in a spot or two, but in the proles, who have remained human throughout. And it is significant that the descriptions of the proles in *Nineteen Eighty-Four* are echoes of the descriptions of ordinary English men and women in Orwell's earlier works, including *The English People*, a book written for the Britain in Pictures Series. The proles, Winston believes, will someday build a better world. And Winston's faith in the proles is an echo of Orwell's faith in the ordinary Englishman. The subtitle of *The Lion and the Unicorn* is "Socialism and the English Genius."

In *Nineteen Eighty-Four* Absolute Compliance Is Demanded

Alfred Kazin

Alfred Kazin was a highly regarded American writer, educator, and literary critic. Among his works are On Native Grounds *and* Bright Book of Life. *Kazin's politics were generally considered more moderate than those of other New York City intellectuals in his circle, many of whom were socialists.*

George Orwell created the nightmare world of Nineteen Eighty-Four *to vent his outrage over political events of the day, ranging from massive unemployment to the attraction Marxism had for many members of the British left-wing intelligentsia. Central themes in* Nineteen Eighty-Four *are the tyranny of the state over its citizens, language stripped of all meaning, and the eradication of history and the past. The power of tyrants is frightening, Kazin asserts in the following viewpoint, because tyranny allows for no dissent and insists it has the perfect answer.*

In [1984] thirty rocket bombs a week are falling on the capital; nothing more is said of them. Like the "atombomb" that explodes over Oceania's "Airstrip I"—England—and by destroying a church provides a hiding place in the belfry for the lovers in an "almost deserted stretch of country," all these bombs are abstractions in a book that, except for the hardships of daily living borrowed from the 1940s, is meant to be an abstract of a wholly political future. Orwell was an efficient novelist not particularly interested in fiction; he used it for making a point. Bombs in *1984* symbolize Orwell's pent-up

Alfred Kazin, "Not One of Us," *The New York Review of Books*, vol. 31, June 14, 1984, pp. 13–14, 16, 18. Copyright © 1984 by NYREV, Inc. Reprinted with permission from The New York Review of Books.

rage about everything in the political world from the mass unemployment of the 1930s (which continued well into the war period) to the ignorance of the left intelligentsia justifying Stalinism because the Russian people were pouring out their blood. By 1948, when Orwell was finishing the novel he had conceived in 1943, he was also maddened by the postwar division of the world, the atom bombs on Japan, and England's dependency on America. The ex-radical neoconservative proponents of America-as-ideology now trying to claim Orwell overlook the fact that England's currency in *1984* is American. England is Oceania Airstrip I. We know whose airstrip it is.

A World with No Meaning

Winston Smith and his fellows in the Ministry of Truth spend their days rewriting the past: "Most of the material you were dealing with had no connection with anything in the real world, not even the kind of connection that is contained in a direct lie." Not Orwell's novel is fiction but the world itself. Fiction as deliberate abstraction from life is what this terror society lives on. By political fiction Orwell means a society that has no meaning. A collectivized insanity is what a wholly tendentious politics has reduced us to. *We* have become the vacuum. Appearance has replaced reality, and appearance is just propaganda. In this future emptiness any two of the three great powers dividing the world (Orwell was grimly sure there would soon be two) may be officially but only symbolically at war. This is a war without end, because it is probably being waged in the "Ministry of Peace." Or if it is really going on, like the present war between Iran and Iraq [1980–88], the belligerents may not recall why they went to war. Truckloads of enemy prisoners are regularly shown to London, but they may not be prisoners or even enemies. Bombs do occasionally fall on the city, but like [Nicaraguan president Anastasio] Somoza or [Syrian president Mafezal] Assad the rulers of this society probably bomb their own people to keep them cowed.

By V-E [Victory in Europe] Day more than ten thousand rocket bombs had fallen on Britain; it would have been knocked out of the war if the enemy's bases had not been captured in time. The thirty bombs falling each week in *1984* are symbols of the routine terror that Orwell imagined for the end of the century. Politics for him had become the future as complete domination. Pervasive injustice had certainly become his vision of things. In *1984* only the utter disregard of the masses by the Party (a theme fundamental to the book but not demonstrated as fully as the devastation of language and the elimination of the past) shows Orwell's compassion struggling against his shuddering vision of the future. "Work and bed," I used to hear English factory workers complain. "Might as well be dead." The deadly fatigue of 1939–1945 is captured in one line about Winston Smith's neighbor Mrs. Parsons. "One had the impression that there was dust in the creases of her face."

What Orwell would not transfer from 1945 to 1984 was the positive and liberating aspect of wartime controls. England was in many respects more fully mobilized for war than Nazi Germany. A general improvement in national health and social services convinced many people that such efficiency called for widespread nationalization. An impatient drive for a better life increasingly filled the atmosphere as Germany finally went down to defeat. To the amazement of many people in the "movement," this brought the Labour party to power with the greatest majority in the history of British socialism. Orwell's writings of the period reflect little of this. It is true that he was ailing with the lung disease that was to kill him in 1950, that his wife Eileen had died in March 1945 when he was in Germany as a correspondent, that he was still writing for the left-wing *Tribune*. It is also true that the author of the wickedly brilliant satire on Stalinism, *Animal Farm*, continued to proclaim himself a supporter of the Labour party and a libertarian Socialist.

Nevertheless, the bread-and-butter issues that brought Labour to power did not get into the novel that made Orwell's name a symbol for the fear of socialism. The tyranny in this book is called "Ingsoc," English Socialism. Like so many Americans on the left, Orwell was more concerned with what Russia portended for socialism than with the actual struggles of the working class. "Socialism" in America is just a rumpus between nostalgic and former radicals. In England it was a national movement, a government in power, an aroused consciousness. What was more on Orwell's mind, despite his undiminished sympathy for Labour, was the issue of domination which he knew so well from his upper-class background, though he derived, he said, from the lower part of it. Or as [Russian revolutionary Vladimir] Lenin put it, Who Whom?—who's going to run the show and drive the rest of us?

Socialism Was a Moral Issue

Socialism to George Orwell, as to the utopian reformers and idealists of the nineteenth century, was not an economic question but a moral one. The welfare state little interested Orwell. He was naive, or perhaps just literary, when he wrote in *The Road to Wigan Pier*, his documentary of British poverty in the Thirties, "economic injustice will stop the moment we want it to stop, and no sooner, and if we genuinely want it to stop the method adopted hardly matters." To the twenty-six-year-old Karl Marx writing in the *Economic and Philosophical Manuscripts* (1844), the purpose of socialism was to end, for once in human history, the economic struggle for existence that has always kept man from "reappropriating" his essence. Exactly a century later Orwell wrote in a book review, "The real problem of our time is to restore the sense of absolute right and wrong when the belief that it used to rest on—that is, the belief in personal immortality—has been destroyed. This demands faith, which is a different thing from credulity."

Just at the moment when twentieth century technology had shown itself capable of feeding the hungry, when everything in sight justified Marx's testimony in *The Communist Manifesto* to the power of new productive forces and [English philosopher Alfred North] Whitehead's praise of "the century of hope" for "inventing invention," socialism in its original meaning—the end of tribal nationalism, of man's alienation from his own essence, of wealth determining all values in society—yielded to the nightmare of coercion. What drove Orwell into an opposition all his own, what made for the ominousness of *1984*, for a deadliness of spirit that fills the book and helped to kill him at forty-six, was his inability to overlook the source of the nightmare. Lenin had seized the state in the name of the long-suffering working class. Thomas Hobbes in 1651 had called Leviathan "the mortal God." He ascribed its power over men to their fear of violent death at each other's hands in the brute state of nature. Fear causes men to create a state by contracting to surrender their natural rights and to submit to the absolute authority of a sovereign. By the social contract men had surrendered their natural liberties in order to enjoy the order and safety of the organized state. But under the total domination of the socialist state men could be just as afraid of violent death at each other's hands as they had been in the state of nature. . . .

Hostile critics of *1984* have eagerly picked on the fact that despite his attempt to immerse himself in workingclass life, Orwell did not commit himself to socialism until he returned to England in 1937, after being wounded in the Spanish Civil War and hunted by Loyalist police for having fought with the proscribed anti-Stalinist POUM [Workers' Party of Marxist Unification]. It was the wonderful fraternalism of the anarchists and other obstinate idealists on the left that gave Orwell his one image of socialism as a transformation of human relationships. In Catalonia, for a brief season after [Francisco] Franco's revolt in 1936, the word "comrade" really meant something. In *Homage to Catalonia* Orwell recited with wonder the disappearance of the usual servility and money worship. What a glorious period that was—until the nominally socialist government in Madrid, instigated by the communists, frustrated every possibility of social revolution from within. Even before Franco conquered in 1939, the old way of life had been restored in Catalonia.

Orwell never forgot what he had seen in Catalonia. This was more than "socialism with a human face," it was socialism as true and passionate equality. Socialism, he wrote near the end of his life, can mean nothing but justice and liberty. For Orwell socialism was the only possible terminus—where? when?—to the ceaseless deprivations suffered by most human beings on earth. But since he equally abominated the despotisms still justified by many English and American left intellectuals, he made a point in *1984* of locating the evil in the thinking of the leading Thought Policeman, O'Brien.

Political intellectuals on the left, the ex-left, the would-be left, the ideological right, can be poison. By the time he summed up all his frustration and rage in *1984*, Orwell had gone beyond his usual contempt for what he called "the boiled rabbits of the left." He was obsessed by the kind of rationale created by modern intellectuals for tyranny by the state. O'Brien's speeches to the broken Winston Smith in the Thought Police's torture chamber represent for Orwell the core of our century's political hideousness. Although O'Brien says that power seeks power and needs no ideological excuse, he does in fact explain to his victim what this power is.

Disbelief Is a Threat to Power

The power exerted and sought by political intellectuals is that they must always be right. O'Brien is frightening because of the way he thinks, not because of the cynicism he advances. [Fyodor] Dostoevsky in *The Possessed* said of one of his revolutionist "devils"—"When he was excited he preferred to risk

A movie poster promoting Michael Anderson's 1956 film adaptation of Orwell's 1984, in which an oppressive government monitors citizens' every move. Hulton Archive/Getty Images.

anything rather than to remain in uncertainty." O'Brien tells his victim: "You are a flaw in the pattern, Winston. You are a stain that must be wiped out. . . . It is intolerable to us that an erroneous thought should exist anywhere in the world, however secret and powerless it may be."

Every despotism justifies itself by claiming the power of salvation. Before salvation by the perfect society, there was salvation by the perfect God. One faction after another in history claims to represent perfection, to the immediate peril of those who do not. My salvation cannot tolerate your disbelief, for that is a threat to my salvation.

O'Brien tortures Winston Smith because of O'Brien's necessary belief that the mind controls all things. There is in fact no external reality. The world is nothing but man and man nothing but mind. Winston, not yet electro-shocked into agreeing to this, protests from his rack: "The world itself is only a speck of dust. And man is tiny—helpless! How long has he been in existence? For millions of years the earth was uninhabited." O'Brien: "Nonsense. The earth is as old as we are, no older. How could it be older? Nothing exists except through human consciousness. . . . Before man, there was nothing. After man, if he could come to an end, there would be nothing. Outside man there is nothing."

That is the enemy in 1984, and against it the exhausted and dying English radical, in the great tradition of English common-sense empiricism, is putting forth his protest that the world is being intellectualized by tyrants who are cultural despots. They are attempting to replace the world by ideas. They are in fact deconstructing it, emptying it of everything that does not lend itself to authority which conceives itself monolithically, nothing but consciousness.

George Orwell's explicitly old-fashioned view is that reality does start outside of us; it is in fact political. Because we are never really alone, whatever introspection tells us, power is always exerted in the name of what we have in common. Life is lived, little as some of us recognize it, as manufactured and coercive loyalties, unmistakable threats and terrible punishments, violent separations from the body politic. The sources of social control and domination are swallowed up in our anxiety, which in an age of psychology deludes itself as being wholly personal, and are embedded in a consumer society professing the elimination of all wants and having no other goal but satisfaction. Actually, we are creatures of society, which is why the tyrant state arises in answer to some mass deprivation. Then the tyranny that afflicts us in our name attempts to reconstitute us by forces so implacable that we internalize them. This is the aim of the Party in *1984*.

Subconscious Compulsion

Nineteen Eighty-Four is in one respect an exception to the methodical social documentation that was Orwell's usual method. The most powerful details in the book relate to our identification with compulsion. The book is a prophecy, or, as Orwell said, a warning about a future terrible because it rests on a fiction and so cannot be substantiated. It would never occur to Orwell's unwearied enemy on the British left, Raymond Williams, that every pious mouthful he still utters about "Socialism" is the merest abstraction couched in the in-house vocabulary of a religious sect. Orwell's attack on O'Brien as the Grand Inquisitor of an enforced solipsism has not been widely understood. Unlike nineteenth-century individualists, who still had some perspective on the society that was forming around them, we no longer recognize the full extent of the social controls *for* which we more and more live. Orwell would have enjoyed the irony. Our media culture confirms [Albert] Einstein's belief that the history of an epoch is represented by its instruments. Yet nothing in the sensationalist discussion of Orwell's novel has been so mindless as television's pointing with alarm at the telescreen in *1984* peeking into our bedrooms. You would think that the telescreen had invented itself.

Orwell had the peculiar ability to show that social coercion affects us unconsciously. It becomes personal affliction. In *Down and Out in Paris and London* and in *The Road to Wigan Pier* he showed poverty not just as destitution but as the crippling of the spirit. In *Homage to Catalonia* and in *1984* he demonstrated the extent to which a state at war must hold its own people hostage. What is not abstract in *1984* is that Winston and Julia make love under the eyes of the State, that Winston in the Ministry of Truth rewrites the past, day after day, all day long, and flogs himself to work only with the help of the Victory Gin given out at lunch with the watery stew and ersatz bread. Winston and Julia make love to the sounds of a proletarian woman in the yard singing as she does her wash. But the moment the lovers are arrested, "Something was being dragged across the stones. The woman's singing had stopped abruptly. There was a long, rolling clang, as though the washtub had been flung across the yard, and then a confusion of angry shouts which ended in a yell of pain." . . .

Part of a Great Tradition

Orwell admitted that he was too ill when writing *1984* to round it all out. But of course it succeeds, it threatens, it terrorizes, because it represents a wholly oppositionist point of view that calls for the downright and repeated emphases of the great pamphleteer rather than the subtly developing action within a novel. Orwell's marked tendency to directness, flatness, laying down the law, along with his powerful anticipation of fact, belongs to a radical and adversary tradition of English pamphleteering not practiced by American writers—the tradition of [Jonathan] Swift, Tom Paine, [William] Hazlitt, [William] Blake, [William] Cobbett, [G.K.] Chesterton, [George Bernard] Shaw, founded on some enduring sense of injustice, on the need to break through those English class prejudices that Orwell called "a curse that confronts you like a wall of stone." Edmund Wilson used to say that the English

Revolution took place in America. In Britain literature has been the revolution. Orwell represents this for the first half of [the twentieth] century as none of his countrymen do. As always, the revolution stays in just one head at a time.

Nevertheless, the great pamphleteers are the great issue raisers. Issues became Orwell's writing life, which is why even when he was near death he could never resist accepting still another book for review. His "I Write as I Please" column for the *Tribune* makes up the central section of his work; the four volumes of his collected essays, letters, journalism are more interesting to me than his novels. *Nineteen Eighty-Four*, novel or not, could have been conceived only by a pamphleteer who in his migratory life insisted on keeping his extensive collection of English pamphlets. His way of writing is always more or less an argument. He writes to change your mind. Socialism, which had meant justice and liberty, in its regression now forced him to choose liberty in *1984* as the response of "the last man in Europe" (the original title for the book) to the State's organized atrocities against a man alone.

But that is not the whole story behind *1984*, as Orwell bitterly insisted, just before he died, against all those attempting to turn him into a defender of the system he described in *The Road to Wigan Pier*. "We are living in a world in which nobody is free, in which hardly anybody is secure, in which it is almost impossible to be honest and to remain alive. . . . And this is merely a preliminary stage, in a country still rich with the loot of a hundred years. Presently there may be coming God knows what horrors—horrors of which, in this sheltered island, we have not even a traditional knowledge." Rosa Luxemburg, the critic on the left most trenchant on Lenin's despotism, warned before she was murdered in 1919 that true victory lay "not at the beginning but at the end of revolution." The true radicals are those who conceive the beginning but cannot bear the end. Ignazio Silone as an exile in Switzerland used to lament: "We are the anti-fascists, always anti! anti!"

Orwell's problem was no doubt that, like so many of us, he knew best what he was against. All the more reason to take him seriously at a time when it has become unfashionable and even dangerous to be "against."

Nineteen Eighty-Four Warns of the Post–World War II Threats to Personal Liberty

Robert F. Gleckner

Robert F. Gleckner was a professor of English at Duke University and the author of Byron and the Ruins of Paradise.

Nineteen Eighty-Four *is often taught as a dystopian novel foretelling a totalitarian future and alerting readers to the dangers of Soviet communism; however, as Gleckner explains in the following selection, George Orwell's message is that the world of 1948, the time when he was writing his novel, already was displaying alarming perils to individual liberty, and those perils were not limited to Soviet nations. Gleckner asserts that* Nineteen Eighty-Four *is Orwell's wake-up call to jolt Western nations out of complacency and to show them that the threats to their liberties were present within their own systems.*

George Orwell's *1984* is taught in a number of universities, usually with particular emphasis upon its relationship to Utopiah and anti-Utopian fiction. As a teacher of the novel I have found that such an approach can be misleading if two other important points are neglected: (1) that the novel is not a frightening prophecy, and (2) that it is not merely an attack upon the Soviet system (as is *Animal Farm*, for example). Students, the general reading public, and an alarming number of critics and commentators do not seem to see that 1984 is in reality 1948 (the year of the book's composition), or for us, 1956; and hence, while acknowledging its horror and its science-fiction realism, they consider the novel merely an ex-

Robert F. Gleckner, "1984 or 1948?" *College English*, vol. 18, no. 2, November 1956, pp. 95–99.

traordinarily competent [H.G.] Wellsian prophecy in Soviet Russian terms. To some extent such a reading of *1984* has been discouraged by recent, more objective criticism of the book, like that of [Richard J.] Voorhees, [Laurence] Brander, and [George] Woodcock. But among students, particularly, the more superficial reading prevails. This may be partly the result of a kind of mass-conditioning of the student mind by the very mass media, junk reading, and advertising soporifics which Orwell attacks in all of his writings; but it is also the result of the students' relative ignorance of present conditions in Russia and China especially. While the average reader of *1984* is probably vaguely aware of attacks upon his own privacy (physical, intellectual, and moral), and while the recent publicity about brain-washing, the rewriting of [Joseph] Stalin's career, and television "monitors" in jails, schools, and nurseries has probably reinforced his general belief about totalitarian or authoritarian methods, his limited access (or desire for access) to certain books and periodicals leaves him still sceptical about Orwell's Newspeak, for example, or double-think, or the suppression of sex. . . .

Orwell Satirizes Control of Thought

The struggle for freedom of feeling is a major theme in *1984*. For Julia, a member of the Anti-Sex League, the simple physical act of sex is rebellion, her individual defiance of the state; for Winston his love for Julia comes to constitute the one inviolable corner of his private soul—until that too is invaded in Room 101. In an extremely pertinent article, "Sex in the Soviet Union," Miss Vera Sandomirsky establishes the fundamental reality of Orwell's vision of a de-eroticized society. As she puts it, the idea of Soviet virtue "means first the de-erotization [*sic*] of love and, secondly, the subordination of the sexual drive to the political and economic exigencies of the Soviet State. But there still remains a third aspect, . . . the most sinister of all: its use as a device for invading the one sphere of personal privacy yet remaining to the Soviet citizen." A recent example of this appeared in *Life* a picture story of a young Soviet married couple, both state-subsidized students, who, because of the exigencies of their work; do not live together.

Yet despite the frightening implications of an anti-sex program, Orwell's most devastating satire is directed against the totalitarian control of human thought to the point where individual thought will be impossible. . . . "Newspeak," Orwell writes, "was designed not to extend but to *diminish* the range of thought. . . . The intention was to make speech . . . as nearly as possible independent of consciousness." Each reduction in the vocabulary "was a gain, since the smaller the area of choice, the smaller the temptation to take thought. Ultimately it was hoped to make articulate speech issue from the larynx without involving the higher brain centers at all."

This seems to be precisely what the Chinese Communists have in mind. As [Fritz] Van Briessen reveals . . . in the Peiping (and presumably other Chinese Communist) newspapers "the number of strokes in ideograms, which frequently are over twenty, has been reduced to—sometimes—only five or six. . . ." Though this is not the first attempt to "reform" the Chinese language and its seventy-odd recognized dialects, the reason for the Communists' determination is clear. It is the same reason that prompted Big Brother to institute Newspeak. James D. White explained this reason, and some of the language reform program. . . . The basic idea is to substitute a phonetic alphabet for the 250,000 or so Chinese ideographs used in the written language "because the ancient characters contain easily recognized concepts of human relationships evolved in pre-Communist China which are intolerable to the Communists." . . .

Orwell Warns Against Complacency

That Orwell's *1984* is not merely a terrifying prophecy, then, can be fairly easily demonstrated. As he himself wrote in his notebook, "Where I feel that people like us understand the situation better than so-called experts is not in any power to

A poster from BBC TV's production 1984 *shows government's threat to citizens' liberties while under the watchful eye of Big Brother.* Larry Ellis/Express/Hulton Archive/Getty Images.

fore-tell specific events, but in the power to grasp what *kind* of world we are living in." But that world is not limited to Soviet Russia or Communist China; and Orwell's satire is not merely of Communism. His "most vital theme," as Woodcock points out, "is the defeat of conscience" everywhere. Orwell uses the Russian state as a model simply because, as satirist, he wants to present the failings of our world in their most fully developed form, as [Jonathan] Swift did in *Gulliver's Travels*, [Aldous] Huxley in *Brave New World*, [Samuel] Butler in *Erewhon*. To read *1984* only as an attack on Russia is to assume the very attitudes against which Orwell fought all his life—smugness, complacency, intellectual laziness, and lack of self-awareness. To counteract such attitudes, one can do no better than to reread an essay like "Politics and the English Language" in the light of *1984*. In that essay Orwell writes, for example:

> When one watches some tired hack on the platform mechanically repeating the familiar phrases—*bestial atrocities, iron heel, bloodstained tyranny, free peoples of the world, stand shoulder to shoulder*—one often has a curious feeling that one is not watching a live human being but some kind of dummy: a feeling which suddenly becomes stronger at moments when the light catches the speaker's spectacles and turns them into blank discs which seem to have no eyes behind them. And this is not altogether fanciful. A speaker who uses that kind of phraseology has gone some distance towards turning himself into a machine. The appropriate noises are coming out of his larynx, but his brain is not involved as it would be if he were choosing his words for himself. If the speech he is making is one that he is accustomed to make over and over again, he may be almost unconscious of what he is saying. . . . And this reduced state of consciousness, if not indispensable, is at any rate favorable to political conformity.

This passage, including the vivid eyeglass image, is used almost verbatim to describe the babbling party member in the canteen scene of *1984*. There Orwell concludes, "The stuff that was coming out of him consisted of words, but it was not speech in the true sense: it was a noise uttered in unconsciousness, like the quacking of a duck." In the essay Orwell makes the point explicit, and applicable to all men everywhere: "This invasion of one's mind by ready-made phrases ... anesthetizes a portion of one's brain."

Other sources could be cited, but these seem to me sufficient to show that by eliminating the prophetic, science-fiction label attached to *1984* and by realizing the applicability of its terrors to our own lives, we can see more clearly that Orwell's fear was not merely of a totalitarian overthrow of the free world, but of an obscuring and dimming and ultimately an elimination of objective truth in all countries. And he saw this coming about not only through force, but because of the moral and intellectual obliquity of the average man.

Nineteen Eighty-Four Is About the Misuse of Power

Julian Symons

Although Julian Symons was best known as a British crime writer, he was also a biographer, literary critic, poet, and author of social and military history, including Between the Wars.

In this excerpt, which was an influential review of Nineteen Eighty-Four *shortly after its publication, Symons calls the work a serious study of power and corruption. For Symons, the work is flawed by a "schoolboyish sensationalism," such as in the scene in Room 101. George Orwell, on reading the review, wrote Symons to thank him for his positive comments and for pointing out the weakness in his novel.*

It is possible to make a useful distinction between novelists who are interested primarily in the emotional relationships of their characters and novelists for whom characters are interesting chiefly as a means of conveying ideas about life and society. It has been fashionable for nearly half a century to shake a grave head over writers who approach reality by means of external analysis rather than internal symbolism; it has even been suggested that the name of novelist should be altogether denied to them. Yet it is a modern convention that the novel must be rather visceral than cerebral. The novel in which reality is approached through the hard colours of outward appearance (which is also, generally, the novel of ideas) has a respectable lineage, and distinctive and distinguished modern representatives. Among the most notable of them is Mr. George Orwell; and a comparison of *Nineteen Eighty-Four*, his new story of a grim Utopia, with his first novel *Burmese Days*

Julian Symons, "Power and Corruption," *The Times Literary Supplement*, June 10, 1949, p. 380. Copyright © 1949 by The Times Supplements Limited. Reproduced from The Times Literary Supplement by permission.

... shows a curious and interesting journey of the mind. It is a queer route that Mr. Orwell has taken from Burma to the Oceania of *Nineteen Eighty-Four*, by way of Catalonia and Wigan Pier.

An Awful Plausibility

It is natural that such a writer as Mr. Orwell should regard increasingly the subject rather than the form of his fictional work. *Burmese Days* is cast fairly conventionally in the form of the contemporary novel; this form had almost ceased to interest Mr. Orwell in 1939, when, in *Coming Up For Air* the form of the novel was quite transparently a device for comparing the England of that time with the world we lived in before the First World War. In *Coming Up For Air*, also, characterization was reduced to a minimum; now, in *Nineteen Eighty-Four*, it has been as nearly as possible eliminated. We are no longer dealing with characters, but with society.

The picture of society in *Nineteen Eighty-Four* has an awful plausibility which is not present in other modern projections of our future. In some ways life does not differ very much from the life we live to-day. The pannikin of pinkish-grey stew, the hunk of bread and cube of cheese, the mug of milkless Victory coffee with its accompanying saccharine tablet—that is the kind of meal we very well remember; and the pleasures of recognition are roused, too, by the description of Victory gin (reserved for the privileged—the "proles" drink beer), which has "a sickly oily smell, as of Chinese rice-spirit" and gives to those who drink it "the sensation of being hit on the back of the head with a rubber club." We can generally view projections of the future with detachment because they seem to refer to people altogether unlike ourselves. By creating a world in which the "proles" still have their sentimental songs and their beer, and the privileged consume their Victory gin, Mr. Orwell involves us most skillfully and uncomfortably in his story, and obtains more readily our belief in the fantasy of thought-domination that occupies the foreground of his book.

In *Nineteen Eighty-Four* Britain has become Airstrip One, part of Oceania, which is one of the three great world-States. The other two are Eurasia and Eastasia, and with one or the other of these States Oceania is always at war. When the enemy is changed from Eurasia to Eastasia, the past is wiped out. The enemy, then, has always been Eastasia, and Eurasia has always been an ally. This elimination of the past is practised in the smallest details of administration; and incorrect predictions are simply rectified retrospectively to make them correct. When, for instance, the Ministry of Plenty issues a "categorical pledge" that there will be no reduction of the chocolate ration, and then makes a reduction from thirty grammes to twenty, rectification is simple. "All that was needed was to substitute for the original promise a warning that it would probably be necessary to reduce the ration at some time in April." The appropriate correction is made in *The Times*, the original copy is destroyed, and the corrected copy placed on the files. A vast organization tracks down and collects all copies of books, newspapers and documents which have been superseded. "Day by day and almost minute by minute the past was brought up to date."

The State Aims for Thought Control

To achieve complete thought-control, to cancel the past utterly from minds as well as records, is the objective of the State. To this end a telescreen, which receives and transmits simultaneously, is fitted into every room of every member of the Party. The telescreen can be dimmed but not turned off, so that there is no way of telling when the Thought Police have plugged in on any individual wire. To this end also a new language has been invented, called "Newspeak," which is slowly displacing "Oldspeak"—or, as we call it, English. The chief function of Newspeak is to make "a heretical thought—that is, a thought diverging from the principles of Ingsoc (English Socialism in Oldspeak)—literally unthinkable." The word "free," for example, is still used in Newspeak, but not in the sense of "politically free" of "intellectually free," since such conceptions no longer exist. The object of Newspeak is to restrict, and essentially to order, the range of thought. The end-objective of the members of the Inner Party who control Oceania is expressed in the Newspeak word "doublethink," which means:

> To know and not to know, to be conscious of complete truthfulness while telling carefully-constructed lies, to hold simultaneously two opinions which cancelled out, knowing them to be contradictory and believing in both of them; to use logic against logic, to repudiate morality while laying claim to it, to believe that democracy was impossible and that the Party was the guardian of democracy; to forget whatever it was necessary to forget, then to draw it back into memory again at the moment when it was needed, and then promptly to forget it again: and, above all, to apply the same process to the process itself.

The central figure of *Nineteen Eighty-Four* is a member of the Outer Party and worker in the records department of the Ministry of Truth, named Winston Smith. Winston is at heart an enemy of the Party; he has not been able to eliminate the past. When, at the Two Minutes' Hate sessions the face of Emmanuel Goldstein, classic renegade and backslider, appears on the telescreen mouthing phrases about party dictatorship and crying that the revolution has been betrayed, Winston feels a hatred which is not—as it should be—directed entirely against Goldstein, but spills over into heretical hatred of the Thought Police, of the Party, and of the Party's all-wise and all-protecting figurehead, Big Brother.

Winston's heresy appears in his purchase of a beautiful keepsake album which he uses as a diary—an activity likely to be punished by twenty-five years' confinement in a forced labour camp—and in his visits to the "proles" areas, where he tries unsuccessfully to discover what life was like in the thirties and forties. He goes to the junk shop where he found the album and buys a glass paper-weight; and he is queerly moved by the old proprietor's quotation of a fragment of a forgotten nursery rhyme: "Oranges and lemons, say the bells of St. Clement's." Sexual desire has been so far as possible removed from the lives of Party members; and so Winston sins grievously and joyously with Julia, a member of the Junior Anti-Sex League.

The downfall of Winston and Julia is brought about through O'Brien, a friendly member of the Inner Party, who reveals that he, too, is a heretic. They are admitted to membership of Goldstein's secret organization "the Brotherhood," which is committed to the overthrow of the Party. But O'Brien is not in fact a member of "the Brotherhood"—if indeed that organization is not simply an invention of the Inner Party—and the benevolent-seeming proprietor of the junk shop belongs to the Thought Police. 'Winston is arrested and subjected by O'Brien to physical and mental coercion; its effect is to eradicate what O'Brien calls his defective memory. The past, O'Brien tells him, has no real existence. Where does it exist? In records and in memories. And since the Party controls all records and all memories, it controls the past. At last Winston is converted to this view—or rather, his defective memory is corrected. Our last sight of Winston shows him sitting in the Chestnut Tree café, haunt of painters and musicians. A splendid victory has been announced, and Winston hears of it not with scepticism but with utter belief. He looks up at the great poster of Big Brother.

> Two gin-scented tears trickled down the sides of his nose. But it was all right, everything was all right, the struggle was finished. He had won the victory over himself. He loved Big Brother.

The corrosion of the will through which human freedom is worn away has always fascinated Mr. Orwell; *Nineteen*

Eighty-Four elaborates a theme which was touched on in *Burmese Days*. Flory's criticism of Burma might be Winston Smith's view of Oceania: "It is a stifling, stultifying world in which to live. It is a world in which every word and every thought is censored. . . . Free speech is unthinkable." And Flory's bitter words: "Be as degenerate as you can. It all postpones Utopia," is a prevision of Winston saying to Julia in his revolt against Party asceticism: "I hate purity, I hate goodness! I don't want any virtue to exist anywhere." But in *Nineteen Eighty-Four* the case for the Party is put with a high degree of sophistical skill in argument. O'Brien is able easily to dispose of Winston in their discussions, on the basis that power is the reality of life. The arrests, the tortures, the executions, he says, will never cease. The heresies of Goldstein will live for ever, because they are necessary to the Party. The Party is immortal, and it lives on the endless intoxication of power. "If you want a picture of the future, imagine a boot stamping on a human face—for ever."

Power and Corruption

Mr. Orwell's book is less an examination of any kind of Utopia than an argument, carried on at a very high intellectual level, about power and corruption. And here again we are offered the doubtful pleasure of recognition. Goldstein resembles [Leon] Trotsky in appearance, and even uses Trotsky's phrase, "the revolution betrayed"; and the censorship of Oceania does not greatly exceed that which has been practised in the Soviet Union, by the suppression of Trotsky's works and the creation of "Trotskyism" as an evil principle. "Doublethink," also, has been a familiar feature of political and social life in more than one country for a quarter of a century.

The sobriety and subtlety of Mr. Orwell's argument, however, is marred by a schoolboyish sensationalism of approach. Considered as a story, *Nineteen Eighty-Four* has other faults (some thirty pages are occupied by extracts from Goldstein's book, *The Theory and Practice of Oligarchical Collectivism*): but none so damaging as this inveterate schoolboyishness. The melodramatic idea of the Brotherhood is one example of it; the use of a nursery rhyme to symbolize the unattainable and desirable past is another; but the most serious of these errors in taste is the nature of the torture which breaks the last fragments of Winston's resistance. He is taken, as many others have been taken before him, to "Room 101." In Room 101, O'Brien tells him, is "the worst thing in the world." The worst thing in the world varies in every case; but for Winston, we learn, it is rats. The rats are brought into the room in a wire cage, and under threat of attack by them Winston abandons the love for Julia which is his last link with ordinary humanity. This kind of crudity (we may say with Lord Jeffrey) will never do; however great the pains expended upon it, the idea of Room 101 and the rats will always remain comic rather than horrific.

But the last word about this book must be one of thanks, rather than of criticism: thanks for a writer who deals with the problems of the world rather than the ingrowing pains of individuals, and who is able to speak seriously and with originality of the nature of reality and the terrors of power.

Nineteen Eighty-Four Promotes the Values of the Common People

Stephen Ingle

Writing extensively on the relationship between politics and literature, Stephen Ingle is head of the Department of Politics at the University of Stirling in Scotland. He is also the author of numerous books, among them The Social and Political Thought of George Orwell.

In the following selection, Ingle asserts that George Orwell's theme in Nineteen Eighty-Four *and in other works is that totalitarianism is not just a political system but is, at its heart, a state of mind. Orwell was not writing to warn of the totalitarian dangers lurking in fascism—those dangers were only too obvious. Rather, Ingle states, he wanted to shake his fellow socialists out of their complacency to the danger that totalitarianism could take root within socialism and in Britain.*

Although it is widely recognised that Orwell's Spanish experiences led him to question the integrity of some left-wing intellectuals, especially communists and fellow-travellers, it should be remembered that his battle with the intellectuals was of older origins. In his Eton days, it will be recalled, he was spoken of as liking to present himself as the 'new [George] Bernard Shaw' and we are told that he had read all of the works of Shaw and H.G. Wells. They were his heroes and they were socialists. They were also intellectuals.

Distrust of Left-Wing Intelligentsia

History has written a part for the Fabians [members of a British intellectual socialist movement] as benevolent ladies and

Stephen Ingle, *George Orwell: A Political Life*. Manchester University Press, 1993. Copyright © Stephen Ingle 1993. Reproduced by permission.

gentlemen whose great achievement was to moderate and make respectable the Edwardian socialist movement. There is, in fact, a pronounced disparity between the Fabian myth and its reality. Critics like Leonard Woolf, who have helped to propagate the drawing-room socialist-myth of respectability and moderation can have read little history, beyond that written by Fabians. Their major polemicists, such as Shaw, the Webbs [Sidney and Beatrice] and Wells, were not democrats in the normal sense of the word. Indeed their temper was highly élitist. It was the Fabians, after all, who set up the London School of Economic and Political Science (LSE) precisely to produce the well-trained élite that would, like some modern class of Platonic [after Greek philosopher Plato] guardians, rule in the interests of all. 'Socialism without experts,' said Shaw, 'is as impossible as . . . dentistry without experts'. And we should not misunderstand Shaw, who once declared himself to be a national socialist before Hitler was born; his heroes and heroines are for the most part men and women of action who command and expect to be obeyed, and his definition of democracy: 'a social order aiming at the greatest available welfare for the whole population'. Socialism was not about giving power to the people. No Fabian would do that, said Shaw unless 'his real objective were to achieve a *reductio ad absurdum* [reduction to the absurd] of democracy and have done with it forever'. So for the Fabians socialism was a kind of castor oil to be forced between the teeth of a reluctant working class by a kind and intelligent middle-class health visitor. Small wonder that Shaw and a number of leading Fabians were strong supporters of [Soviet leader Joseph] Stalin and of Soviet communism. When Orwell identified these socialist intellectuals as his enemies, he was not being paranoid.

I have said that Orwell also believed that totalitarianism was at root not a political system but a state of mind. This is a theme which dominated a lot of his writing during the early war years. . . .

Orwell's theme [of an essay titled "Raffles and Miss Blandish"], wrote [German writer] Gollo Mann, is that 'totalitarian danger lies within ourselves and in all the political systems of our time'. But towards the end of the *No Orchids* essay, Orwell went a stage further in specifically associating British intellectual socialists with the desire for power just as he had described it here. There is an interconnection, he argued, between sadism, nationalism, success worship and totalitarianism. 'I believe no one has ever pointed out the sadistic element in Bernard Shaw's work, still less suggested that this probably has some connection with Shaw's admiration for dictators.' Countless British intellectuals, says Orwell, who 'kiss the arse' of Stalin are no different from those who gave allegiance to [Adolf] Hitler and [Benito] Mussolini, nor indeed to [Thomas] Carlyle, [Edward Shepherd] Creasy and others in the nineteenth century who so admired the achievements of Prussianism. Orwell was anxious to establish that this cult of power tends to be mixed up with a love of cruelty for its own sake. He concluded that the English-language tradition of heroes fighting against the odds was now out of date, and Jack the Giant Killer ought to be renamed Jack the Dwarf Killer. Did Orwell know that Bernard Shaw had indeed suggested what he thought was a more appropriate theme for a modern nursery fable: Giant the Jack Killer? Orwell had, in fact, long been concerned with the propensity for 'vicarious bullying' of intellectuals, who he wrote in 1931, tended to believe in 'some vast world-purpose, unquestionably good, and that great men (meaning *successful* men) are its instruments'. It is also clear from other things that he wrote that Orwell had come to dislike Shaw especially. . . . Intellectuals were bullies, then, and intellectual socialists among the worst.

If Orwell wanted to get this message across to socialists generally it was no wonder that he attracted the opprobrium of a number of socialist intellectuals: indeed *Nineteen Eighty-Four* was reviewed in one communist journal under the heading 'Maggot of the month', and the reaction of the radical student in Saul Bellow's *Mr Sammler's Planet* indicates that he had not been forgiven more than twenty years later. 'Orwell was a fink,' he says. 'He was a sick counter-revolutionary. It was good he died when he did.' Even such a perceptive critic as the socialist intellectual Raymond Williams could not forgive Orwell's attacking totalitarianism through the example of *socialist* totalitarianism (or indeed revolution through the example of a socialist revolution). It would have been easy enough for Orwell to have avoided these charges had he wanted to, but the point is precisely that he was writing to praise and not to bury socialism! His readers, or more correctly those for whom he was writing, did not need to be told that fascism was by its nature totalitarian; had not a world war just been fought for this very reason? They did not need to be told that many foreign regimes with an authoritarian disposition could easily slip into totalitarian ways; had not pre-war history shown that all too clearly? But what the insular British left *did* need to be told was that totalitarianism could be built by a socialist regime and that even Britain, with its long and distinguished tradition of liberal values, could provide the home for a totalitarian polity. Orwell wrote *Nineteen Eighty-Four* within the British socialist tradition to warn fellow socialists to be on their guard against an intellectual élite which he despised and which he believed to be chiefly interested in power for its own sake.

Power as an End in Itself

The ruling class in *Nineteen Eighty-Four* established itself in Oceania as the consequence of a socialist revolution and it founded a socialist state which presented itself as an organic whole, subsuming the individual interests of all. But this organicism is soon exposed, for society is organised, indeed regimented, solely for the purpose of maximising the self-interest of the ruling group. It is a perversion of Plato's republic, with power ... and not virtue as the rulers' reward. Technology, applied specifically to the science of scrutiny, provides the means for the group's dominance, but the superstructure which it supports assigns a social role to groups with a rigidity unimaginable even in feudal Christendom. Thus Oceanic society comprises 300 million of whom party members make up 45 million (fifteen per cent); of these, six million (two per cent of the whole) belong to the Inner Party and thirty-nine million (the remaining thirteen per cent) to the Outer Party. The eighty-five per cent of the population who do not belong to the Party comprise the proletariat and are not, in the classical sense, citizens of the state at all.

The purpose of this rigid hierarchy is not immediately apparent and the novel's hero, Winston Smith, wrote in his diary that although he understood *how* the Inner Party retained its control of the state he did not understand *why*; it was clearly no longer motivated by socialist ideology. The purpose of the hierarchy was finally explained to Winston by his interrogator O'Brien as being simple—power. O'Brien defines power not as a means to obtain some end (equality or justice for example) but an end in itself. He argues that no group ever seizes power with the intention of giving it up later. Dictatorships are not set up in order to defend the revolution; rather the revolution is organised to set up a dictatorship. Power is not a means, it is an end. O'Brien goes on to define power: power is being exercised when one individual forces his or her own view of reality upon another, and in a most specific way.

'How does one man assert his power over another, Winston?'

Winston thought. 'By making him suffer', he said.

'Exactly. By making him suffer. Obedience is not enough. Unless he is suffering, how can you be sure that he is obeying your will and not his own? Power is in inflicting pain and humiliation. Power is in tearing human minds to pieces and putting them together again in shapes of your own choosing.'

The future, O'Brien explains to Winston, consists of the members of the Inner Party maximising power through their relationship with the Outer Party. 'If you want a picture of the future,' says O'Brien, borrowing from [British author] James Hadley Chase, 'imagine a boot stamping on a human face forever.'

This constitutes a theory of power as psychosis, arguing that those who seek political power do so simply to inflict suffering on others. Moreover in order to maximise the satisfaction which the exercise of power brings, it has to be exercised directly. On this basis a playground bully might be said to exercise greater power than a president of the United States, since the satisfactions of inflicting suffering are more immediate and direct. . . .

It would probably suit Orwell's purpose well enough if he could frighten us into understanding two things: that power is an end just as much as a means and that totalitarianism is not rational. Ironically it was the one-time Fabian H.G. Wells himself who warned against allowing a man to appoint himself as your shepherd, for sooner or later you would find a crook [of a shepherd's staff] around your ankle. As for the second, Orwell clearly regarded it as important to explore the associated myth of totalitarian rationality. He criticises H. G. Wells for depicting history as a struggle between science and planning on the one hand and disorderly reaction on the other. The truth of the matter was quite a different thing: 'The order, the planning, the state encouragement of science, the steel, the concrete, the aeroplanes, all are there, but all in the service of ideas appropriate to the Stone Age. Science is fighting on the side of superstition.' Again, power, shown to be atavistic and irrational, is the *end*, and scientific rationality only a *means*.

No Privacy in Oceania

The new social order of Oceania in which all pretence is stripped away allows the Inner Party to maximise power, its sadistic satisfaction gained through the suffering of others. Orwell wrote that former civilisations claimed to be founded on love or justice; the Party's order is founded on hatred. In both the old classical theories of the state and that of Oceania, private property and family life have been abolished so that nothing may come between the guardian (Inner Party member) and the state; in Oceania, moreover, all forms of passion not channelled through—indeed directed by—the state are illegal. Orwell says that family life will cease to exist at all in the future, just as in [Aldous] Huxley's *Brave New World*. But whereas with Huxley the power of the sex is diffused, with Orwell it is eradicated: 'We shall abolish the orgasm . . . there will be no loyalty except loyalty to the party.'

It was against this ruling group that Winston pitched himself. He had come to regard himself as the guardian of human values and he sought to maintain these values while recognising from the beginning the inevitability of his eventual defeat. Winston acted against the state by trying to create a private realm—through purchasing and keeping a diary and by indulging in a love affair. He also declared his willingness to act against the state politically. When O'Brien, posing as a leader of the clandestine rebels, the Brotherhood, asked Winston what acts he would be prepared to undertake against the state, Winston agreed to do anything, however devastating its effects upon innocent people. A more crucial point, however, is that Winston's treachery predated this declaration of intent, predated even the purchase of the diary; to question the infallibility of the state within the confines of one's skull was to be doomed—thoughtcrime was treachery. In much the same way that [Arthur] Koestler's Rubashov, in *Darkness at Noon*, nightly expected a visit from the secret police once he began to question the propriety of Number One's policies within the privacy of his own skull, so too Winston knew where his thoughtcrimes would inevitably lead. This lack of a distinction between a private and a public realm is precisely what gives life in Oceania its nightmare quality. Nobody has recourse to a private world in which he or she may regain self-esteem or attempt to control even the smallest part of their own destiny; there is no escape from Big Brother.

What are the elements of the private realm, denied by the Oceanian state, which allow an individual to be fully human? First, the right to be one's own judge of external reality, to be what [social scientist Hannah] Arendt calls a 'moral man'. In essence it was what [Protestant leader] Martin Luther sought to establish by claiming to have direct access, as it were, to God, and not to require the mediation of the Church. The Party stands firmly against this claim, demanding that the individual be willing to reject the evidence of his or her own senses. Reality is not external, says O'Brien. It is the creation of the human mind. Not the individual mind, which makes mistakes and is mortal, but in the mind of the Party, which is collective and immortal. Whatever the Party holds to be truth *is* truth. It is impossible to see reality except by looking through the eyes of the party. It was also impossible to guess what the party might declare to be reality at some time in the future. Winston conjectures that in the end the Party would declare that two plus two made five and the individual would be required to *believe* it (to *accept* it would not be sufficient). 'It was inevitable that they should make that claim sooner or later: the logic of their position demanded it.' . . .

No Individual Rights in Oceania

Not only was the citizen of Oceania deprived of an autonomous moral status, but also of legal status. There is no law in the state beyond the arbitrary dictates of Big Brother. There are no individual rights whatsoever. 'The State is the Law, the moral law as well as the juridical law. Thus it cannot be subject to any standard, and especially not to the yardstick of civil morality.' But the totalitarian state, according to Arendt, is 'shapeless' and unpredictable. Indeed the state could manipulate reality, even the past. Orwell's Spanish experiences had made him painfully aware of this and Winston's position in the Ministry of Truth gave him even greater opportunity to experience the unmaking and remaking of history: 'All history was a palimpsest,' he said, 'scraped clean and reinscribed as often as was necessary.' In *The Book of Laughter and Forgetting*, [Milan] Kundera, after giving an example of the kind of work in which Winston himself was involved—the air-brushing out from old photographs of discredited influential figures—declares that the individual is as much a rewriter of history as the party. 'People are always shouting they want to create a better future. It's not true. . . . The only reason people want to be masters of the future is to change the past.' It is our past that gives us weight and substance, that provides the shape to our self-conceit. Kundera's character sums Orwell's argument up succinctly: 'The struggle of man against power is the struggle of memory against forgetting.' In Oceania the state controls the past and the individual has no memory. Winston Smith is the last individual in Oceania.

Another prerequisite for full individuality, according to Orwell, is family life. In Oceania family life among Party members has broken down entirely. Inner Party members, it will be remembered, have no family. As for the Outer Party, 'the family had become in effect an extension of the Thought Police. It was a device by means of which everyone could be surrounded night and day by informers who knew him intimately.' The model of Oceanian family life is provided by Winston's near neighbours in Victory Mansions, the Parsons. Parsons himself, than whom a more stalwart anti hearty Party member could not be imagined, was eventually betrayed to the Thought Police by his own daughter. But Parsons' predicament was far from unique. 'It was almost normal for people over thirty to be frightened of their children.' The Party had destroyed love and family loyalties and thus deprived the individual of the sustenance that these provide. One of Winston's most enduring memories was of his mother, dying without reproach so that he might live. This act belonged to a former time 'when there was still privacy, love and friendship, and when the members of a family stood by one another without needing to know the reason'. As a focus for loyalty and love and a bastion of privacy the family was a role that the totalitarian state had needed to smash. . . .

Language Passes on Culture

Next Orwell claimed participation in a cultural background for the individual, who needed to feel part of a tradition which represented his or her beliefs and aspirations and which he or she could hope to pass on to their children. For Orwell the most important part of that tradition was language. It is arguably the case that he attached more importance to the nature and function of language than most political theorists and philosophers.

In Oceania the task of the party philologists, like Syme (a man too creative to survive for long), was systematically to control and restrict vocabulary in the belief that behaviour would thus also be controllable. The linguistic analysts believed that behaviour and indeed consciousness were causally related to the nature and structure of language. Syme's claim is no less ambitious: the more vocabulary contracts, the more the Party will be able to control behaviour. 'Don't you see,' he explains to Winston, 'that the whole aim of Newspeak is to narrow the range of thought? In the end we shall make thoughtcrime literally impossible because there will be no words in which to express it.' . . .

In *Nineteen Eighty-four* Winston attempts to re-establish connections with a vanished culture so as to erect a barrier against the Party. The book he bought as a diary was an elegant, old one with smooth, creamy paper. He bought it in Charrington's junk shop, to which he had been instinctively drawn. Then he bought himself a paperweight, a beautiful piece of crystal but without any use. 'If [the lifestyle of the past] survives anywhere, it's in a few solid objects, with no words attached to them, like that lump of glass there,' Winston remarks. The room above the junk shop which Winston and his lover Julia rented from Charrington is described as 'a world, a pocket of the past where extinct animals could walk'. In such a world Winston became whole again, his nagging leg-ulcer briefly cured. Predictably enough, when the Thought Police finally broke into the room one of them smashed the paperweight on the hearthstone, symbolically breaking all connections with the values of the previous culture, and indeed shattering the 'crystal spirit' which epitomised those values (and which, in Spain, Orwell had believed unbreakable). . . .

The State Controls Emotions

Orwell's next claim for the individual was for a full emotional life. He believed that a totalitarian élite would, sooner or later, seek to control human emotions: indeed, as we know, in Oceania the Party was already at work on abolishing the orgasm. All feelings of passion would henceforth be directed towards the Party and used by the Party. The love of Big Brother represents its positive manifestation, hatred directed either to the external threat of Eastasia or Eurasia; the internal threat of Goldstein and the Brotherhood represents the negative. Julie's great attraction for Winston was her vaunted promiscuity, her simple love of carnal pleasures. When they were first alone in the hazel grove, Winston described Julia's quickly unzipping her clothing and flinging it aside as a gesture which seemed to be annihilating a whole civilisation. He was fully aware of, indeed rejoiced in, the treasonable nature of sexual pleasure. 'Listen,' he says to Julia, 'The more men you've had, the more I love you. . . . I hate purity, I hate goodness! I don't want any virtue to exist anywhere. I want everybody to be corrupt to the bone.' Promiscuity, Winston recognised, would provide 'a force that would tear the Party to pieces'. It is doubtful if Orwell believed that widespread promiscuity was a necessary political virtue, that it would provide a sound basis for a liberal democracy for example. It has to be remembered that he supported promiscuity in much the same way as he supported assassination and other acts of terrorism—as demanded by the times. This is not meant to be a eulogising of sexual licence for its own sake. Indeed, Smith later accuses Julia scornfully of being 'only a rebel from the waist down'. Irving Howe argues that eroticism and not love is the enemy of the state in *Nineteen Eighty-Four*. He is only partly right: in room 101 it is love which is cleansed from Winston.

Orwell also claims material sufficiency as a precondition for a full life for the individual. Winston has some ancestral memory which causes him to reject as unnatural the discomfort, the dirt and the scarcity, of life in Oceania. Man has a right to something better than Victory Mansions with its 'lifts that never work, the cold water, the cigarettes that came to pieces, the food with its strange, evil tastes'; a right to something better than a world in which 'nearly everyone was ugly, and would have been ugly even if dressed otherwise than in the uniform blue overalls'. It was deliberate party policy to maintain a condition of scarcity for all but members of the Inner Party so as to enhance the importance of even minor privileges. The struggle for day-to-day necessities, says Orwell, wears down the human spirit and denies individuality.

Orwell Cherished Privacy

Lastly Orwell argues for the importance of individual privacy, for the existence of a private world into which a person could securely retire. It was the *privateness* of the British way of life which Orwell cherished. A home of your own to do what you like in. That was why 'the most hateful of all names in an English ear is Nosey Parker'. But Oceania's telescreens make privacy impossible and because Big Brother might be watching, people are obliged to walk about with an expression of quiet optimism; the portrayal of any other emotion could be construed as treason. The temple of privacy is, as we have seen, inside the skull, and Orwell wanted to make it plain that the temple was no longer sacrosanct. The human being, he wrote in 1944, is not autonomous. [Daniel] Defoe could never actually have written *Robinson Crusoe* on a desert island, nor could any philosopher, scientist or artist exist in isolation; 'they need constant stimulation from other people, it is about impossible to think without talking'. So: by taking away freedom of speech and by weakening the desire for intellectual freedom through socialisation, the space inside the skull becomes not a temple of privacy and liberty but a void. Simply stated, this need for privacy is nothing less than a *sine qua non* [a condition without which it could not be] for a full life for the individual.

The right and capacity to form one's own judgement on external events; a rich and sustaining family life, cultural continuity, based upon a vibrant language, a full emotional life, a life of reasonable material sufficiency and finally a completely private world into which one could retire: these were the bastions of identity which Winston Smith sought to defend. The obliteration of the private realm, the elimination of personal and cultural identity so that nothing stood between the atomised individual and the state: this was the programme of the Party.

Winston's revolt ends in total defeat. On the final page of the novel we find him remade, whole and unalienated for the first time in his adult life, reflecting on his futile struggle:

> O cruel, needless misunderstanding! O stubborn, self-willed exile from the loving breast! Two gin-scented tears trickled down the side of his nose. But it was alright, the struggle was finished. He had won a victory over himself. He loved Big Brother.

Nineteen Eighty-Four Remains Relevant

Nineteen Eighty-Four has had a considerable influence on post-war political thinking. With the collapse of the Soviet Union its influence should remain just as strong, for it stands as a warning of what a modern technological world might be like without the political values which Orwell cherished. It stands as a warning as to which values must be defended if a reasonable life is to remain available to the individual in the next millennium. It stands as a warning to socialists and progressives (and indeed to radical conservatives) that leaders must never be allowed to lose touch with the values of the rank-and-file. It provides a yardstick with which we can measure the extent to which our atomised, technological, mass-communications-based, observer (perhaps voyeur) society is heading for the world of Big Brother and the Party. If *Nineteen Eighty-Four* seems an exaggerated impossibility, [Christopher] Small reminds us that the Nazi's final solution to the 'Jewish problem' had already been parodied over two hundred and fifty years before, by Swift's Houyhnhnms [race of intelligent horses in *Gulliver's Travels*] debating the final solution of the Yahoo [vile and primitive creatures in *Gulliver's Travels*] problem—to expel them from the 'arse-hole of the world'.

Nineteen Eighty-Four
Warns of the Dehumanization
of Industrialism

Erich Fromm

Erich Fromm was an internationally known social psychologist, psychoanalyst, and author whose many works include Escape from Freedom *and* The Art of Loving. *A founder of the socialist humanist movement, he joined the Socialist Party of America in the 1950s.*

In the following selection, Fromm explains that George Orwell's Nineteen Eighty-Four, *Aldous Huxley's* Brave New World, *and Yevgeny Zamiatin's* We *form a trilogy of negative utopias that show that despite the progress people have made, they have created a world that threatens to destroy their humanity. For Orwell, Fromm argues, a fundamental contradiction exists between democracy and the capacity to wage atomic war, a contradiction he introduces through "doublethink." For all three authors, Fromm asserts, the rise of the industrial state has created a culture that has the potential to dehumanize. Only by recognizing the danger, Orwell warns in* Nineteen Eighty-Four, *can it be averted.*

George Orwell's *1984* is the expression of a mood, and it is a warning. The mood it expresses is that of near despair about the future of man, and the warning is that unless the course of history changes, men all over the world will lose their most human qualities, will become soulless automatons, and will not even be aware of it.

The mood of hopelessness about the future of man is in marked contrast to one of the most fundamental features of

Western thought: the faith in human progress and in man's capacity to create a world of justice and peace. This hope has its roots both in Greek and in Roman thinking, as well as in the Messianic concept of the Old Testament prophets. The Old Testament philosophy of history assumes that man grows and unfolds in history and eventually becomes what he potentially is. It assumes that he develops his powers of reason and love fully, and thus is enabled to grasp the world, being one with his fellow man and nature, at the same time preserving his individuality and his integrity. Universal peace and justice and the goals of man, and the prophets have faith that in spite of all errors and sins, eventually this "end of days" will arrive, symbolized by the figure of the Messiah.

The prophetic concept was a historical one, a state of perfection to be realized by man within historical time. Christianity transformed this concept into a transhistorical, purely spiritual one, yet it did not give up the idea of the connection between moral norms and politics. The Christian thinkers of the late Middle Ages emphasized that although the "Kingdom of God" was not within historical time, the social order must correspond to and realize the spiritual principles of Christianity. The Christian sects before and after the Reformation emphasized these demands in more urgent, more active and revolutionary ways. With the breakup of the medieval world, man's sense of strength, and his hope, not only for individual but for social perfection, assumed new strength and took new ways.

One of the most important ones is a new form of writing which developed since the Renaissance, the first expression of which was Thomas More's *Utopia* (literally "Nowhere"), a name which was then generically applied to all other similar works. Thomas More's *Utopia* combined a most penetrating criticism of his own society, its irrationality and its injustice. with the picture of a society which, though perhaps not perfect, had solved most of the human problems which sounded insoluble to his own contemporaries. What characterizes Thomas More's *Utopia*, and all the others, is that they do not speak in general terms of principles, but give an imaginative picture of the concrete details of a society which corresponds to the deepest longings of man. In contrast to prophetic thought, these perfect societies are not at "the end of the days" but exist already—though in a geographic distance rather than in the distance of time.

Thomas More's *Utopia* was followed by two others, the Italian friar Campanella's *City of the Sun*, and the German humanist Andreae's *Christianopolis*, the latter being the most modern of the three. There are differences in viewpoint and in originality in this trilogy of utopias, yet the differences are minor in comparison with what they have in common. Utopias were written from then on for several hundred years, until the beginning of the twentieth century. The latest and most influential utopia was Edward Bellamy's *Looking Backward*, published in 1888. Aside from *Uncle Tom's Cabin* and *Ben Hur*, it was undoubtedly the most popular book at the turn of the century, printed in many millions of copies in the United States, translated into over twenty languages. Bellamy's utopia is part of the great American tradition as expressed in the thinking of Whitman, Thoreau, and Emerson. It is the American version of the ideas which at that time found their most forceful expression in the socialist movement in Europe.

This hope for man's individual and social perfectibility, which in philosophical and anthropological terms was clearly expressed in the writings of the Enlightenment philosophers of the eighteenth century and of the socialist thinkers of the nineteenth, remained unchanged until after the First World War. This war, in which millions died for the territorial ambitions of the European powers, although under the illusion of fighting for peace and democracy, was the beginning of that development which tended in a relatively short time to destroy a two-thousand-year-old Western tradition of hope and to transform it into a mood of despair. The moral callousness of the First World War was only the beginning. Other events followed: the betrayal of the socialist hopes by Stalin's reactionary state capitalism; the severe economic crisis at the end of the twenties; the victory of barbarism in one of the oldest centers of culture in the world—Germany; the insanity of Stalinist terror during the thirties; the Second World War, in which all the fighting nations lost some of the moral considerations which had still existed in the First World War; the unlimited destruction of civilian populations, started by Hitler and continued by the even more complete destruction of cities such as Hamburg and Dresden and Tokyo, and eventually by the use of atomic bombs against Japan. Since then the human race has been confronted with an even greater danger—that of the destruction of our civilization, if not of all mankind, by thermonuclear weapons as they exist today and as they are being developed in increasingly frightful proportions.

Most people, however, are not consciously aware of this threat and of their own hopelessness. Some believe that just because modern warfare is so destructive, war is impossible; others declare that even if sixty or seventy million Americans were killed in the first one or two days of a nuclear war, there is no reason to believe that life would not go on as before after the first shock has been overcome. It is precisely the significance of Orwell's book that it expresses the new mood of hopelessness which pervades our age before this mood has become manifest and taken hold of the consciousness of people.

Orwell is not alone in this endeavor. Two other writers, the Russian Zamiatin in his book *We*, and Aldous Huxley in his *Brave New World*, have expressed the mood of the present, and a warning for the future, in ways very similar to Orwell's. This new trilogy of what may be called the "negative utopias" of the middle of the twentieth century is the counterpoint to the trilogy of the positive utopias mentioned before, written in the sixteenth and seventeenth centuries [It should be added that Jack London's *The Iron Heel*, the prediction of fascism in America, is the earliest of the modern negative utopias]. The negative utopias express the mood of powerlessness and hopelessness of modern man just as the early utopias expressed the mood of self-confidence and hope of post-medieval man. There could be nothing more paradoxical in historical terms than this change: man, at the beginning of the industrial age, when in reality he did *not* possess the means for a world in which the table was set for all who wanted to eat, when he lived in a world in which there were economic reasons for slavery, war, and exploitation, in which man only sensed the possibilities of his new science and of its application to technique and to production—nevertheless man at the *beginning* of modern development was full of hope. Four hundred years later, when all these hopes are realizable, when man *can* produce enough for everybody, when war has become unnecessary because technical progress can give any country more wealth than can territorial conquest, when this globe is in the process of becoming as unified as a continent was four hundred years ago, at the very moment when man is on the verge of realizing his hope, he begins to lose it. It is the essential point of all the three negative utopias not only to describe the future toward which we are moving, but also to explain the historical paradox.

The three negative utopias differ from each other in detail and emphasis. Zamiatin's *We*, written in the twenties, has more features in common with *1984* than with Huxley's *Brave New World*. *We* and *1984* both depict the completely bureaucratized society, in which man is a number and loses all sense of individuality. This is brought about by a mixture of unlimited terror (in Zamiatin's book a brain operation is added eventually which changes man even physically) combined with ideological and psychological manipulation. In Huxley's work the main tool for turning man into an automaton is the application of hypnoid mass suggestion, which allows dispensing with terror. One can say that Zamiatin's and Orwell's examples resemble more the Stalinist and Nazi dictatorships, while Huxley's *Brave New World* is a picture of the development of the Western industrial world, provided it continues to follow the present trend without fundamental change.

In spite of this difference there is one basic question common to the three negative utopias. The question is a philosophical, anthropological and psychological one, and perhaps also a religious one. It is: can human nature be changed in such a way that man will forget his longing for freedom, for dignity, for integrity, for love—that is to say, can man forget that he is human? Or does human nature have a dynamism which will react to the violation of these basic human needs by attempting to change an inhuman society into a human one? It must be noted that the three authors do not take the simple position of psychological relativism which is common to so many social scientists today; they do not start out with the assumption that there is no such thing as human nature; that there is no such thing as qualities essential to man; and that man is born as nothing but a blank sheet of paper on which any given society writes its text. They do assume that man has an intense striving for love, for justice, for truth, for solidarity, and in this respect they are quite different from the relativists. In fact, they affirm the strength and intensity of these human strivings by the description of the very means they present as being necessary to destroy them. In Zamiatin's *We* a brain operation similar to lobotomy is necessary to get rid of the human demands of human nature. In Huxley's *Brave New World* artificial biological selection and drugs are necessary, and in Orwell's *1984* it is the completely unlimited use of torture and brainwashing. None of the three authors can be accused of the thought that the destruction of the humanity within man is easy. Yet all three arrive at the same conclusion: that it is possible, with means and techniques which are common knowledge today.

Orwell's Thoughts on Atomic War

In spite of many similarities to Zamiatin's book, Orwell's *1984* makes its own original contribution to the question, How can human nature be changed? I want to speak now about some of the more specifically "Orwellian" concepts.

The contribution of Orwell which is most immediately relevant for the year 1961 and for the next five to fifteen years is the connection he makes between the dictatorial society of *1984* and atomic war. Atomic wars had first appeared as early as the forties; a large-scale atomic war broke out about ten years later, and some hundreds of bombs were dropped on industrial centers in European Russia, Western Europe, and North America. After this war, the governments of all countries became convinced that the continuation of the war would mean the end of organized society, and hence of their own power. For these reasons no more bombs were dropped, and the three existing big power blocs "merely continued to produce atomic bombs and stored them up against the decisive opportunity which they all believe will come sooner or later." It remains the aim of the ruling party to discover how "to kill several hundred million people in a few seconds without giving warning beforehand." Orwell wrote *1984* before the discovery of thermonuclear weapons, and it is only a historical footnote to say that in the fifties the very aim which was just mentioned had already been reached. The atomic bomb which was dropped on the Japanese cities seems small and ineffective when compared with the mass slaughter which can be achieved by thermonuclear weapons with the capacity to wipe out 90 per cent or 100 per cent of a country's population within minutes.

The importance of Orwell's concept of war lies in a number of very keen observations.

First of all, he shows the economic significance of continuous arms production, without which the economic system cannot function. Furthermore, he gives an impressive picture of how a society must develop which is constantly preparing for war, constantly afraid of being attacked, and preparing to find the means of complete annihilation of its opponents. Orwell's picture is so pertinent because it offers a telling argument against the popular idea that we can save freedom and democracy by continuing the arms race and finding a "stable" deterrent. This soothing picture ignores the fact that with increasing technical "progress" (which creates entirely new weapons about every 5 years, and will soon permit the development of 100 or 1000 instead of 10 megaton bombs), the whole society will be forced to live underground, but that the destructive strength of thermonuclear bombs will always remain greater than the depth of the caves, that the military will become dominant (in fact, if not in law), that fright and hatred of a possible aggressor will destroy the basic attitudes of a democratic, humanistic society. In other words, the continued arms race, even if it would not lead to the outbreak of a thermonuclear war, would lead to the destruction of any of those qualities of our society which can be called "democratic," "free," or "in the American tradition." Orwell demonstrates the illusion of the assumption that democracy can continue to exist in a world preparing for nuclear war, and he does so imaginatively and brilliantly.

Another important aspect is Orwell's description of the nature of truth, which on the surface is a picture of Stalin's treatment of truth, especially in the thirties. But anyone who sees in Orwell's description only another denunciation of Stalinism is missing an essential element of Orwell's analysis. He is actually talking about a development which is taking place in the Western industrial countries also, only at a slower pace than it is taking place in Russia and China. The basic question which Orwell raises is whether there is any such thing as "truth." "Reality," so the ruling party holds, "is not external. Reality exists in the human mind and nowhere else . . . whatever the Party holds to be truth *is* truth." If this is so, then by controlling men's minds the Party controls truth. In a dramatic conversation between the protagonist of the Party and the beaten rebel, a conversation which is a worthy analogy to Dostoyevsky's conversation between the Inquisitor and Jesus, the basic principles of the Party are explained. In contrast to the Inquisitor, however, the leaders of the Party do not even pretend that their system is intended to make man happier, because men, being frail and cowardly creatures, want to escape freedom and are unable to face the truth. The leaders are aware of the fact that they themselves have only one aim, and that is power. To them "power is not a means; it is an end. And power means the capacity to inflict unlimited pain and suffering to another human being." [This definition of power in Erich Fromm, *Escape from Freedom*. Also Simone Weil's definition that power is the capacity to transform a living person into a corpse, that is to say, into a thing.] Power, then, for them creates reality, it creates truth. The position which Orwell attributes here to the power elite can be said to be an extreme form of philosophical idealism, but it is more to the point to recognize that the concept of truth and reality which exists in *1984* is an extreme form of pragmatism in which truth becomes subordinated to the Party. An American writer, Alan Harrington, who in *Life in the Crystal Palace* gives a subtle and penetrating picture of life in a big American corporation, has coined an excellent expression for the contemporary concept of truth: "mobile truth." If I work for a big corporation which claims that its product is better than that of all competitors, the question whether this claim is justified or not in terms of ascertainable reality becomes irrelevant. What matters is that as long as I serve this particular corporation, this claim becomes "my" truth, and I decline to examine whether it is an objectively valid truth. In fact, if I change my job and move over to the corporation which was until now "my" competitor, I shall accept the new truth, that its product is the best, and subjectively speaking, this new truth will be as true as the old one. It is one of the more characteristic and destructive developments of our own society that man, becoming more and more of an instrument, transforms reality more and more into something relative to his own interests and functions. Truth is proven by the consensus of millions; to the slogan "how can millions be wrong" is added "and how can a minority of one be right." Orwell shows quite clearly that in a system in which the concept of truth as an objective judgment concerning reality is abolished, anyone who is a minority of one must be convinced that he is insane.

In describing the kind of thinking which is dominant in *1984*, Orwell has coined a word which has already become part of the modern vocabulary: "doublethink." "*Doublethink* means the power of holding two contradictory beliefs in one's mind simultaneously, and accepting both of them. . . . This process has to be conscious, or it would not be carried out with sufficient precision. But it also has to be unconscious, or it would bring with it a feeling of falsity and hence of guilt." It is precisely the unconscious aspect of doublethink which will seduce many a reader of *1984* into believing that the method of doublethink is employed by the Russians and the Chinese, while it is something quite foreign to himself. This, however, is an illusion, as a few examples can demonstrate. We in the West speak of the "free world" in which we include not only systems like those of the United States and England, which are based on free elections and freedom of expression, but we include also South American dictatorships (at least we did as long as they existed); we also include various forms of dictatorship like those of Franco and Salazar, and those in South Africa, Pakistan and Abyssinia. While we speak about the free world, we actually mean all those states which are against Russia and China and not at all, as the words would indicate, states which have political freedom. Another contemporary example of holding two contradictory beliefs in one's mind simultaneously and accepting them can be found in our discussion about armament. We spend a considerable part of our income and energy in building thermonuclear weapons, and close our minds to the fact that they might go off and destroy one third or one half or most of our population (and that of the enemy). Some go even further; thus Herman Kahn, one of the most influential writers on atomic strategy today, states, "... in other words, war is horrible, there is no question about it, but so is peace, and it is proper with the kind of calculations we are making today to compare the horror of war and the horror of peace, and see how much worse it is."

Kahn assumes that thermonuclear war might mean the destruction of sixty million Americans, and yet he finds than even in such a case "the country would recover rather rapidly and effectively," [H. Kahn] and that "normal and happy lives for the majority of the survivors and their descendants" [H. Khan] would not be precluded by the tragedy of thermonuclear war. This view holds: a) that we prepare for war in order to preserve peace, b) that even if war breaks out and the Russians kill one third of our population and we do the same to them (and if we can, of course, more) still, people will live happy lives afterwards, c) that not only war but also peace is horrible, and it is necessary to examine how much more horrible war is than peace. People who accept this kind of reasoning are called "sober"; those who doubt that if two million or sixty million died it would leave America essentially untouched are not "sober"; those who point to the political and psychological and moral consequences of such destruction are called "unrealistic."

While this is not the place for a lengthy discussion on the problem of disarmament, these examples must be given in order to make the point which is essential for the understanding of Orwell's book, namely that "doublethink" is already with us, and not merely something which will happen in the future, and in dictatorships.

Another important point in Orwell's discussion is closely related to "doublethink," namely that in a successful manipulation of the mind the person is no longer saying the opposite of what he thinks, but he thinks the opposite of what is true. Thus, for instance, if he has surrendered his independence and his integrity completely, if he experiences himself as a thing which belongs either to the state, the party or the corporation, then two plus two are five, or "Slavery is Freedom," and he feels free because there is no longer any awareness of the discrepancy between truth and falsehood. Specifically this applies to ideologies. Just as the Inquisitors who tortured their prisoners believed they acted in the name of Christian love, the Party "rejects and vilifies every principle for which the socialist movement originally stood, and it chooses to do this in the name of socialism." Its content is reversed into its opposite, and yet people believe that the ideology means what it says. In this respect Orwell quite obviously refers to the falsification of socialism by Russian communism, but it must be added that the West is also guilty of a similar falsification. We present our society as being one of free initiative, individualism and idealism, when in reality these are mostly words. We are a centralized managerial industrial society, of an essentially bureaucratic nature, and motivated by a materialism which is only slightly mitigated by truly spiritual or religious concerns. Related to this is another example of "doublethink," namely that few writers, discussing atomic strategy, stumble over the fact that killing, from a Christian standpoint, is as evil or more evil than being killed. The reader will find many other features of our present Western society in Orwell's description in *1984*, provided he can overcome enough of his own "doublethink."

Certainly Orwell's picture is exceedingly depressing, especially if one recognizes that as Orwell himself points out, it is not only a picture of an enemy but of the whole human race at the end of the twentieth century. One can react to this picture in two ways; either by becoming more hopeless and re-signed, or by feeling there is still time, and by responding with greater clarity and greater courage. All three negative utopias make it appear that it is possible to dehumanize man completely, and yet for life to go on. One might doubt the correctness of this assumption, and think that while it might be possible to destroy the human core of man, one would also in doing this destroy the future of mankind. Such men would be so truly inhuman and lacking in vitality that they would destroy each other, or die out of sheer boredom and anxiety. If the world of *1984* is going to be the dominant form of life on this globe, it will mean a world of madmen, and hence not a viable world (Orwell indicates this very subtly by pointing to the mad gleam in the Party leader's eyes). I am sure that neither Orwell nor Huxley or Zamiatin wanted to insist that this world of insanity is bound to come. On the contrary, it was quite obviously their intention to sound a warning by showing where we are headed for unless we succeed in a renaissance of the spirit of humanism and dignity which is at the very roots of Occidental culture. Orwell, as well as the two other authors, is simply implying that the new form of managerial industrialism, in which man builds machines which act like men and develops men who act like machines, is conducive to an era of dehumanization and complete alienation, in which men are transformed into things and become appendices to the process of production and consumption. [This problem is analyzed in detail in Erich Fromm, *The Sane Society.*] All three authors imply that this danger exists not only in communism of the Russian or Chinese versions, but that it is a danger inherent in the modern mode of production and organization, and relatively independent of the various ideologies. Orwell, like the authors of the other negative utopias, is not a prophet of disaster. He wants to warn and to awaken us. He still hopes—but in contrast to the writers of the utopias in the earlier phases of Western society, his hope is a desperate one. The hope can be realized only by recognizing it, so *1984* teaches us, the danger with which all men are confronted today, the danger of a society of automatons who will have lost every trace of individuality, of love, of critical thought, and yet who will not be aware of it because of "doublethink." Books like Orwell's are powerful warnings, and it would be most unfortunate if the reader smugly interpreted *1984* as another description of Stalinist barbarism, and if he does not see that it means us, too.

The Capitalist Past in *Nineteen Eighty-Four* Is Presented Positively

Arthur Eckstein

Arthur Eckstein is an American literary critic.

In the following selection, Eckstein asserts that George Orwell's position as an avowed socialist is hard to reconcile with the attractive picture he paints of the capitalist past and the attack he makes on a collectivized state in Nineteen Eighty-Four. *However, the capitalist past he is referring to is the one of the nineteenth century, when he saw capitalism linked strongly with liberty. By the time he had come to write* Nineteen Eighty-Four, *Eckstein explains, Orwell feared collectivism more than capitalism, for he believed the capitalist system was waning, while collectivism was on the rise. More than a socialist, however, Orwell was a liberal, and he recognized that under capitalism the artist had experienced a golden age. This, more than anything, accounted for his ambivalent attitude toward capitalism.*

To the end of his life, George Orwell remained a socialist. In "Why I Write" (1946), we find his programmatic statement: "Every line of serious work that I have written since 1936 has been written, directly or indirectly, *against* totalitarianism and *for* democratic Socialism, as I understand it." Orwell had fiercely attacked the attitude of capitalist society towards the poor in *Down and Out in Paris and London* (1933) and in *The Road to Wigan Pier* (1937). He always made a point of wearing the blue shirt of the French working class. And in the last summer of Orwell's life (1949) he enrolled his

Arthur Eckstein, "1984 and George Orwell's Other View of Capitalism," *Modern Age*, Winter 1985, pp. 11–19. Copyright © 1985 Intercollegiate Studies Institute Inc. Reproduced by permission.

adopted son Richard in the anarchist colony at Whiteway. Of *1984* specifically, Orwell wrote to Francis Henson: "My recent novel is NOT intended as an attack on Socialism or on the British Labour Party (of which I am a supporter). . . ."

Freedom Existed Under Capitalism in *1984*

Yet if Orwell remained in his own mind a man of the Left (indeed, the far Left), a paradox appears if we survey the references to the capitalist "past" in his last and greatest work. The capitalist "past" of *1984* is, of course, to a great extent Orwell's present. And seen from the nightmare world of Ingsoc [English Socialism], the capitalist "past" has much to recommend it—in fact, just about everything to recommend it.

There are two outstanding characteristics of this vanished "past." First, material life for the average person had been far better in the "past" than under Ingsoc. Examples are numerous: the wide availability of real coffee, real sugar, real chocolate, good beer, wine, fruit, solidly-built furniture, elevators that worked. Above all: the wide availability of well-made books and even objects kept for their intrinsic beauty alone.

Second, in the "past" there had existed individual freedom: freedom of thought, human rights, even freedom of speech. The total suppression of human freedom under Ingsoc is, of course, the main theme of *1984* and needs no detailing. But that such freedom had once existed Orwell is careful in the novel to make clear: we are not dealing here with mere theoretical human possibilities. In the "past," then, it had been usual for people to read books in the cozy and complete privacy of their own homes—without fear of the Thought Police. In the "past" people had kept diaries, to record events and thoughts for themselves: this had been taken for granted. In the "past" human relationships had existed naturally, without constant state interference—which is why the life of intimacy and honesty lived by Winston Smith and Julia above the old junk shop is explicitly called a relic of an earlier age. In the "past" there had been no imprisonment without trial, no public executions, no torture to extract confessions. In the "past" orators espousing all sorts of political opinions had even had their free public say in Hyde Park [park in London famous for its Speakers' Corner].

And from Goldstein's *Book* Orwell's hero Winston Smith learns that the previous existence of relative plenty and relative individual freedom had not come about by accident. Relative plenty had resulted from the increasing use of industrial machines in the late nineteenth and early twentieth centuries, which in turn had led to wider distribution of goods and very greatly increased standards of living. Relative individual freedom had prevailed because:

> The heirs of the French, English and American revolutions had partly believed their own phrases about the rights of man, freedom of speech, equality before the law . . . and had even allowed their conduct to be influenced by them to some extent.

Capitalism, according to the Party, had meant a world of poverty and slavery. In the course of the first part of *1984*, Winston Smith's varied historical research—interviews, the collecting of artifacts, and the reading of Goldstein's *Book*—reveal to him that this is a lie. The capitalist "past" had not been perfect: prosperity and freedom had been only partial. But obviously, the previous capitalist civilization had been beyond measure preferable to the current Ingsoc State. Conversely, Winston comes to see that it is Ingsoc *itself* which is responsible for the current conditions of poverty and slavery.

It is at least in part this "lost civilization" that Winston toasts in the famous scene in which he and Julia are inducted into the (bogus) underground resistance movement:

> "What shall it be this time?" [O'Brien said]. "To the confusion of the Thought Police? To the death of Big Brother? To humanity? To the future?" "To the past," said Winston. "To

the past." Winston's point may partly be to celebrate a past that is in general unalterable and sacrosanct, despite the cynical slogan of the Party on this matter. Perhaps, too, Winston's toast is an indirect expression of Orwell's well-known nostalgia for the English past of his own childhood. However, the most direct reference here seems to be to the specific "lost past" of England before the Ingsoc Revolution—for that is the (capitalist) "past" which Winston throughout the whole first part of the novel has been attempting, with desperate intensity, to rediscover.

Positive View of Capitalism Contradictory

Since Orwell was a socialist, this basically positive depiction of "past" capitalist society in *1984* represents a problem. And the problem is compounded by a closer examination of the Henson letter. Orwell explains, as we noted above, that *1984* is not intended as an attack on socialism; yet in the very next phrase he also says that the book is intended as "a show-up of the perversions to which a centralised economy is liable." Thus, a convinced socialist has written a book in which the effects of a centralized, planned economy are socially disastrous and in which capitalist society appears quite attractive—especially (but not solely) by contrast. The first element here can probably be explained as an outgrowth of Orwell's ongoing dispute in the 1940s with the authoritarian Left—the communists and their supporters within the English intelligentsia. But the second element is even more intriguing, since, strictly speaking, it is unnecessary to the theme of the novel. That is, there was simply no need for Orwell to portray the "past" capitalist world so attractively in order to condemn the brutal totalitarianism of the Ingsoc State. We are dealing here at least partly with an ambivalence—even a contradiction—in Orwell's attitude towards capitalism: or so I will argue. Basically, Orwell despised capitalism; but especially in his most pessimistic moods, he was willing to concede it a crucial virtue.

In Orwell's original forebodings about the destruction of civilization (1933), the engine of destruction would be [Aldous] Huxley's "Fordification": capitalism and consumerism. The population of the world would be reduced to docile wage-slaves, their lives utterly in the hands of "the bankers." Under the impact of the cataclysmic events of the 1930s, however—the coming of [Adolf] Hitler, the Soviet purge trials, his experience in the Spanish Civil War—a different vision eventually began to impose itself on Orwell. By 1938 he was coming to fear that civilization would be destroyed by the worldwide triumph of state dictatorship.

Orwell Appreciated Freedoms

The first truly detailed exposition of Orwell's dark vision of eventual worldwide totalitarianism occurs in his essay on Henry Miller: "Inside the Whale" (written in the summer and autumn of 1939; published in March 1940). In seeking to explain the political quietism of Miller's writing, Orwell argues that an inevitable historical process is leading to the destruction of "western civilization"—which he defines as *laissez-faire* ["let (people) do (as they wish)," meaning government should not intervene in the marketplace] capitalism and liberal-Christian culture. What is coming is the centralized state, and the new world war will only hasten its arrival. But the implications of this development have not been fully understood, Orwell says, because people have falsely imagined that socialism would most likely be a better form of liberalism. On the contrary: "almost certainly we are moving into an age of totalitarian dictatorships," an age in which both freedom of thought and the autonomous individual will be stamped out of existence. But this in turn means that "literature, in the form we have known it, must suffer at least a temporary death"—for literature has depended on the existence of the autonomous individual writer. In the present a writer may well choose to aid the coming of the new age, but he cannot contribute to this political process as a writer, "for *as a writer* he is a liberal, and what is happening is the destruction of liberalism." Hence Henry Miller's political quietism. As a writer—as a liberal—the only honest subject left to him in this age of violent political change is personal life (sex).

In this essay Orwell emphasizes that western literature has depended upon individual freedom of thought, and that both have depended upon the existence of a "liberal-Christian culture"—which is disappearing, in favor of the centralized state. No direct link is made as yet between literature and the existence of capitalism as a specific economic system. There are hints in that direction, but only hints (*laissez-faire* capitalism is paired with liberal-Christian culture as essential to the definition of "western civilization"; and the autonomous, honest writer is described as "a hangover from the bourgeois age"). Nor is Orwell against socialism: the centralized state which is now coming may be grim, but it may also be a grim necessity. This is why Orwell allows writers to participate in the struggle to bring about the new world (although, he emphasizes, not as writers). And Orwell does not completely abandon hope that this new world might eventually produce its own great literature (of a new sort, it is true). He ends the essay with the assertion that Miller's political quietism demonstrates the impossibility of any major literature "*until* the world has shaken itself into its new shape."

Still, this is only a small ray of light in an otherwise very dark landscape. In fact, Orwell's publisher, Victor Gollancz, a man of strong left-wing views, was upset with "Inside the Whale" and wrote Orwell that he was being too pessimistic about the future. Orwell replied:

> You are perhaps right in thinking I am over pessimistic. It is quite possible that freedom of thought etc. may survive in an economically totalitarian society. We can't tell until a collectivised economy has been tried out in a western country.

But at the moment, Orwell continues, he is more worried about intellectuals stupidly equating British democracy with fascism or despotism: given the current threat from Germany, he hopes that the common people will have more sense.

For us there are three points to note in this important letter. First, Orwell at this time clearly is not fully pessimistic about the effect of a collectivized state on intellectual freedom. Second, we see that Orwell (perhaps at Gollancz's prodding) is indeed exploring in his mind the relationship between freedom of thought and the specific form of *economic* life within a society. And we can see his unease with the idea that society might be both "economically totalitarian" and intellectually free: it is possible, but somehow not logical. Third, Orwell brings Gollancz back from theory to reality, firmly asserting the value of the freedoms currently existing in Britain: capitalist Britain is not a fascist despotism and deserves defending by everyone. This was an idea that set Orwell apart from many leftist intellectuals, and it was still relatively new within Orwell himself. Well into 1939 he had continued to equate British "democracy" with fascism—the position he now castigated in others. But with the coming of war with the Nazis, Orwell had experienced a sudden, monumental awakening of sentimental patriotism, and this letter to Gollancz shows that it included an appreciation of the freedoms Britain actually provided. Those freedoms formed the reality against which Orwell would henceforth judge socialist theory. . . .

Fearing the State More than Capitalism

It is . . . striking that after 1941 Orwell occasionally wrote passages extolling nineteenth-century capitalism and capitalist society as phenomena characterized, above all, by human freedom. The most famous instance occurs in "Riding Down to Bangor" (1946). In discussing the mood of certain mid-Victorian American novels, Orwell remarks:

> They have not only innocence but ... a buoyant, carefree
> feeling, which was the product, presumably, of the unheard,
> of freedom and security which nineteenth-century America
> enjoyed. ... [It] was a rich, empty country ... in which the
> twin nightmares that beset every modern man, the night-
> mare of unemployment and the nightmare of State interfer-
> ence, had hardly come into being. ... There was not, as
> there is now, an all-prevailing sense of helplessness. There
> was room for everybody, and if you worked hard you could
> be certain of a living—could even be certain of growing
> rich; this was generally believed, and for the greater part of
> the population it was even broadly true. In other words, the
> civilisation of nineteenth-century America was capitalist
> civilisation at its best.

Such outright praise of anything is rare in Orwell.

Orwell returned more than once to this theme of the nineteenth century as an age of human freedom. And after 1941
we also find occasional brief remarks where he links capitalism directly or indirectly with liberty (especially intellectual
liberty). He praised unregulated, independent small business-
men, too; and he came to use the term "capitalist democracy"
without irony (unusual in a man of the far Left).

This is not to suggest that Orwell's view of capitalism ever
became basically positive. On the contrary. Whatever his occasionally idealizing (and even naive) attitude towards a stage of
capitalism in the past, Orwell feared and despised what he saw
as the giant "monopoly" capitalism of the present. As powerful and as impersonal as the State, it was just as capable of
crushing the individual—through the unemployment line,
rather than the interrogation chamber.

By the early 1940s Orwell had also become deeply suspicious of economic collectivism *per se* [by itself]: especially the
threat it posed to intellectual freedom. As the Henson letter
shows, this suspicion never faded. Similarly, Orwell had come
to fear the implications of the growing power of the State
over society. Indeed, Orwell feared the State more than he

feared capitalism—perhaps because he continued to feel that the capitalist system was dying, while he worried that the age of the State was only beginning. Clearly, it was difficult to reconcile these attitudes with his advocacy of socialism, for socialism inevitably involves some form of economic collectivism, as well as an expansion of government control over society: and Orwell understood his conflict here perfectly well. The difficulty may help account for the general "paleness" of Orwell's prosocialist writing after 1941. It is a fact that it is singularly lacking in concrete and convincing detail either about the shape of a democratic socialist society or how we are to get there. This is particularly true of his proposed Socialist United States of Europe—while in the real world Orwell sided with America (*faute de mieux* [for lack of something better]) in the Cold War and castigated intellectuals who did not do the same. Indeed, after 1941 Orwell's real focus of social concern changed radically: he concentrated his literary energies more and more simply on the defense of civil liberties and intellectual freedom. He had come to see how fragile these things were and from how many directions they were threatened. Orwell's friend T.R. Fyvel now tells us that when the postwar Labour government began nationalization of industry and punitive taxation of incomes—two of the very measures which Orwell himself had proposed in "The Lion and the Unicorn"—Orwell "was not against these measures[!] ... only he had become profoundly suspicious of any extension of state power." How deeply Orwell had changed since the euphoria of 1940. Fyvel believes that Orwell always remained a socialist—and then at the last moment he introduces a crucial qualification: "he was formally a socialist."

As a Writer, Orwell Was a Liberal

If Orwell was "formally a socialist," what was he really? Obviously, a complicated and sometimes self-contradictory human being. Fyvel concludes that more than anything else, Orwell was a pessimist; and this is in line with the final judgment of another of Orwell's friends, Herbert Read. In pointing to the polarity between socialism and pessimism in Orwell's thought, Alex Zwerdling has put Orwell's dilemma this way: although Orwell claimed to retain faith that a democratic socialism could somehow be achieved, his critique of the statist tendencies within the socialist movement was devastating to him, and "a hopeless faith is a contradiction in terms." My point is in a way the reverse of Zwerdling's, but also complements it: Orwell's moods of pessimism made him not only more wary of socialism, but also less hostile to capitalism and capitalist society.

But I would also suggest that besides the polarity of socialism/pessimism, there was another polarity in Orwell's thought. As a political person he was (or considered himself) a socialist, but as a writer he was a liberal. I am not the first to describe Orwell as a liberal; indeed, both George Woodcock and Bertrand Russell even call him a "nineteenth-century liberal." But I mean the term in the specific way Orwell himself used it, the way he felt was vital to a writer: "liberty-loving," especially regarding freedom of thought. Thus, as a writer—as a liberal—Orwell intensely valued liberal and tolerant surroundings, valued the relatively liberal and tolerant surroundings provided by bourgeois England, and feared that economic collectivism would lead to the destruction of liberalism and toleration. I would suggest that this fear which Orwell felt as a writer eventually came to balance the ideals of "social justice" and economic equality which he upheld as a (democratic) socialist. This goes a long way towards explaining the special emphasis in *1984* on the destruction of autonomous thought by the Party, the emphasis on the (collectivist) economic origins of Ingsoc society, and, conversely, the novel's depiction of pre-revolutionary capitalist society as basically benign.

But, of course, socialist and writer were one man. And Orwell himself was well aware of the fundamental ambivalence into which he had fallen:

> If one thinks of the artist as ... an autonomous individual who owes nothing to society, then the golden age of the artist was the age of capitalism. He had then escaped from the patron and had not yet been captured by the bureaucrat. ... Yet it remains true that *capitalism, which in many ways was kind to the artist and the intellectual generally,* is doomed and is not worth saving anyway. So you arrive at these two antithetical facts: (1) Society cannot be arranged for the benefit of artists; (2) without artists civilisation perishes. I have not yet seen this dilemma solved (there must be a solution), and it is not often that it is honestly discussed.

"There must be a solution": Orwell offers none here, and one may wonder whether he ever found one. The best he seems to have been able to come up with, actually, was advocacy of a human "change of heart"—an argument of desperation. At least he honestly discussed the problem (as he saw it) of the potentially profound conflict between intellectual freedom and economic centralization. It is this dilemma, I think, which lies at the origin of Orwell's "other" view of capitalism.

Orwell's Private Nightmare Proved Prophetic

T.R. Fyvel

A close friend of Orwell, T.R. Fyvel was an author, journalist, broadcaster, and the coeditor of Searchlight Books.

In the following selection, Fyvel writes that George Orwell takes the elements of his own personal nightmares—his phobias about rats, images of a boot on a face, the deprivations of wartime— and creates in Nineteen Eighty-Four *an allegory that warned of the dangers of a totalitarian future. Orwell was remarkably prescient, Fyvel asserts. For example, Orwell's image of "a boot stamping on a human face—forever" was played out in Communist Czechoslovakia and in the campaign against the Solidarity movement in Poland.*

It is fair to say that Orwell's last work has, more than any book published since 1945, subtly affected the popular impression of the way history has been proceeding. The book contains obvious elements of his private nightmare—the hero's loneliness and guilt, memories of London's wartime squalor, his phobia about rats, images of a boot on a face . . . And yet, out of his *private* nightmare Orwell by his supreme effort produced a book profoundly and prophetically related to the *public* problems of the time, an allegory that after his death has become like a measuring rod of history.

This impact is all the more remarkable because at first sight, as one reads it today, *Nineteen Eighty-Four* has a few very evident faults. True, the imaginary future Orwell wrote about back in 1948 still has a very ingenious look—he had good insight into the shape of history to come. The world of 1984 which Orwell drew was dominated by three totalitarian superstates—Eurasia (Soviet Union), Eastasia (communist China) and Oceania (the US) and for a writer looking ahead in 1948 this was not a bad guess. He saw Britain as Oceania's Airstrip One—again not a bad guess, but then the American connection simply drops out of his story, leaving Britain alone as a totalitarian Oceania. As such, in Orwell's picture, it is ruled to the last detail by the all-powerful Party, which is headed by Orwell's nice invention of a mythical protector, Big Brother, the fount of all wisdom and virtue—and of absolutely total ruthlessness. (Well, we have since Orwell's death seen the temporary rise of some similar figures.) The Party is divided into the mysterious privileged minority of the Inner Party and Orwell's chosen victims (his own social class), the harassed Outer Party members who are constantly watched over by the Thought Police for deviation, dissenters being tortured within the Ministry of Love and vaporized.

In this coherent inferno, the watching is done through ubiquitous telescreens—Orwell's single mechanical invention for the future—through which the Party simultaneously broadcasts lying propaganda and has everybody watched all the time for possible heresy. (Again, this is not a bad broad forecast of today's mounting Government supervision of citizens by computer storage of information.)

But now we come to the Proles, the vast working-class majority of the population who do not count in Orwell's Britain of 1984; and here he seemed to stumble. His picture is of a completely demoralized British working class:

> The Proles were born, they grew up in the gutters, they went to work at twelve, they passed through a brief blossoming period of beauty and sexual desire, they married at twenty, they were middle-aged at thirty, they died, for the most part, at sixty. Heavy physical work, the care of home and

children, petty quarrels with neighbours, films, football, beer, and above all, gambling filled up the horizon of their minds.

This picture has not only little connection with the real organized and motorized British workers of the eighties, taking their holidays in Florida; it was an old-fashioned view even at the time when Orwell wrote in 1948. Since he severely censured Kipling for writing patronizing poems about soldiers who dropped their aitches, his own laboured attempts to reproduce Prole cockney speech are curious. Altogether, it is odd that Orwell, when writing on Jura in 1948, should in his Proles produce a picture of the British workers that looks like one taken from his childhood. Other faults in the book strike the reader. Orwell presents his totalitarian Party as deliberately unideological, neither nationalist nor Communist, which seems unlikely. His dirty, run-down London of 1984 with its bomb gaps is no city of the future but the bombed wartime London he remembered. The sinister canteen in the Ministry of Truth where the hero Winston eats is obviously based on the innocent wartime canteen of the BBC, which he also remembered.

And so on. Yet these faults hardly matter. The point is that the reader is soon caught by the sheer power and cohesion of Orwell's nightmare vision of a savage, totalitarian society— above all, one in which nothing can change. Orwell's Party rules Oceania by a system of *doublethink* under which two opposed opinions can be held simultaneously. Thus, while it derides every principle of English socialism, Orwell has the Party call its philosophy 'Ingsoc'. In the name of Ingsoc, under the Party's *doublethink*, London is forever dominated by the skyscrapers of the Ministry of Truth, where lies are fabricated, the Ministry of Love, where prisoners are tortured by the Party, and the Ministry of Plenty, which arranges strict food rationing. Within the nightmare, life is forever unchanged. The clocks of London strike thirteen. Big Brother glares from giant posters and his eyes watch the citizens through the telescreens. In his cubicle in the Ministry of Truth, the hero Winston Smith sits forever changing and falsifying past copies of *The Times* in keeping with current Party edicts, because the Party maintains that whoever controls the past controls the future. Every day, there takes place the two minutes' hate, during which the always defeated, yet equally undying traitor Goldstein appears hatefully on the telescreen, until pushed away by Big Brother. In the canteen Winston's colleague Simes is too knowing and so is vaporized by the Thought Police—it is inevitable. Life is shabby, the streets of London are shabby but Party parades are held in their full glory—Winston's girl Julia marches regularly in the ranks of the Anti-Sex League.

Into this nightmarish vision of the future, in which all details dovetail, Orwell has as it were projected himself into the story in the shape of his wretched hero Winston Smith. Whereas in Orwell's other novels the ending is implicit in the telling, Winston's doom is conveyed *explicitly* from the start. He is described as knowing himself doomed when he defies Party rules to keep an individual diary. Doom comes nearer to him and his girl Julia when they start to have an affair. It becomes inevitable when they visit Inner Party member O'Brien and offer to join the traitor Goldstein's army. When arrested, Winston is tortured and brainwashed by O'Brien within the Ministry of Love. His final and ultimate doom arrives when he is taken to room 101 'where the worst thing in the world happens', the worst thing in Winston's case being that a cage of rats is placed over his face, whereat he collapses, totally recants and becomes an automaton, loving Big Brother. . . .

When composing *Nineteen Eighty-Four*, he was touching on the problems of very real dictatorship while writing in the horrendous dictatorial age of Hitler, Stalin and others. With a tremendous, exhausting psychological effort, adding no doubt elements of his private nightmare, he tried through the experiences with which he endowed the hapless Winston Smith to look deeply into the collectivist future he saw ahead. As I have said, his immediate model for his totalitarian Oceania was Stalin's Soviet Union, but I think his vision was much wider. As he wrote in the book, by the fourth decade of the twentieth century, all the main currents of political thought were authoritarian. The earthly paradise had been discredited at exactly the moment when it had seemed, through technology, to become realizable. These words in *Nineteen Eighty-Four* are put into the mouth of the rebel Goldstein, but there is no reason to think they are not Orwell's own. In previous writings he had stressed that bourgeois individuality was going, the bonds of family, locality, religion, craft and profession were going. In their place a new collectivism was spreading in society, whether in work or life or leisure. But it also appeared to Orwell in 1948 that the new collective did not bring the earthly paradise any nearer. Not only that, it appeared to him that under the threat of violence and the nuclear terror, the new collective could become grotesquely dehumanized. It is as a permanent warning against the danger of the dehumanized collective in our society that *Nineteen Eighty-Four* has survived and should be seen to have survived.

Two concluding points. When Orwell told me that because he thought ill health had affected it, he was dissatisfied with *Nineteen Eighty-Four* (he wrote to Julian Symons that he had 'ballsed it up') I think that his dissatisfaction was mainly directed at the third part of the book, where Winston is interrogated and tortured by O'Brien. From my first reading, one passage had particularly remained in my mind, that in which O'Brien explains that to Big Brother and the Party, power and the infliction of torture on victims are not only justified for their own sake. They are also justified for ever.

> "If you want a picture of the future, imagine a boot stamping on a human face—forever . . ."

> "And remember that it is forever. The face will always be there to be stamped upon. The heretic, the enemy of society,

will always be there, so that he can be defeated and humiliated over again ... The espionage, the betrayals, the arrests, the tortures, the executions, the disappearances will never cease."

I remember how at my first reading I had thought that here Orwell was really piling on his private nightmare a bit, yet the words must have made an impact on readers and been specially remembered. I found the passage used as comment in articles on the tenth anniversary of the Soviet crushing of Dubcek's liberal Communist Czech régime and on the twenty-fifth anniversary of the Soviet crushing of the Hungarian revolution; and on the occasion of the crushing of Solidarity in Poland in 1981–2, I found it said in the press that to Comrade Brezhnev, the Soviet boot must be on the face of the satellite countries forever. Like other Orwellian sayings, it has proved to be prophetic.

My last point concerns the Appendix on 'Newspeak'. The American Book of the Month Club at first wanted him to omit it. Fortunately he resisted, for his account of how his Party rulers in Oceania were busy eliminating large numbers of common English words from existence and substituting newly knocked-up words for others in order to make heretical thought impossible—this is almost the best touch of satire in the whole book. It is hard to resist the temptation to quote Orwell's own eloquent example of the substitution by the Party of new words for old to stop heretical thought:

> Consider, for example, such a typical sentence from a *Times* leading article as *Oldthinkers unbellyfeel Ingsoc*. The shortest rendering that one could make of this in Oldspeak would be: "Those whose ideas were formed before the Revolution cannot have a full emotional understanding of the principles of English Socialism." But this is not an adequate translation. To begin with, in order to grasp the full meaning of the *Newspeak* sentence quoted above, one would have to have a clear idea of what is meant by *Ingsoc*. And, in addi-

tion, only a person thoroughly grounded in Ingsoc could appreciate the full force of the word *bellyfeel* which implies a blind, enthusiastic acceptance difficult to imagine today; or of the word *oldthink*, which was inextricably mixed up with the idea of wickedness and decadence.

I noticed how in her splendid autobiographical account of her political imprisonment under Stalin, the Soviet author Eugenia Ginzburg referred to Orwell's comments on totalitarian society with an apparent certainty that her references would be understood. When I mentioned this to a Russian friend—well, she was lucky enough to have come out of the Soviet Union five years ago—she said: 'What do you mean? With his *Newspeak* and *Doublethink*. Orwell wrote for us! No Westerner could understand him as intimately as we in the Soviet Union felt he understood our lives.'

Orwell Accused the Leftist Intelligentsia of Abuse of Power in *Nineteen Eighty-Four*

John David Frodsham

John David Frodsham is Foundation Professor of Comparative Literature at Murdoch University, Western Australia.

In the following selection, Frodsham asserts that, although George Orwell remained a socialist, he became deeply distrustful of the left-wing intelligentsia, whom he felt had subverted the ideals of democracy to their own lust for power. He wrote Nineteen Eighty-Four *to warn against the disasters that he foresaw. Orwell also feared the dehumanizing effects of technology, Frodsham states. His message was a clear one—resist Marxism and machines, or accept a totalitarian society.*

Orwell's greatness lies in his moral stature, while his peculiar contribution to modern literature lies in his application of morality, of the dictates of unsilenced conscience, to the politics of our bloody and murderous era.

Orwell Is a Controversial Novelist

I have said that *1984* is a great novel and Orwell a major writer. Not everyone, however, would agree with me. His name has long been anathema in the Soviet Union and its satellites as well as in China, where it has long been banned. It is unlikely, I feel, that the work will ever be translated into Cambodian or Vietnamese, or that it will circulate widely in official circles in Cuba, Albania or North Korea. Nor for that matter,

John David Frodsham, "The New Barbarians: Totalitarianism, Terror, and the Left Intelligentsia in Orwell's *1984*," *World Affairs*, vol. 147, Winter 1984–1985, pp. 139–60. Copyright © 1984–1985 by Helen Dwight Reid Educational Foundation. Reproduced with permission of the Helen Dwight Reid Educational Foundation, published by Heldref Publications, 1319 18th Street, NW, Washington, DC 20036-1802.

is it likely to be prescribed reading for schools in Paraguay or Haiti; for Big Brother is a creation of the Right as well as of the Left and is every bit as fascist as he is communist. It is noteworthy that, in the West, the Marxist intelligentsia, who increasingly dominate our universities, respond angrily to praise of Orwell who, to them, is (to quote a contemporary novelist [Saul Bellow, in his *Mr. Sammler's Planet*]) "a fink and a sick counter-revolutionary". Some of our literary mandarins [bureaucrats], too, have sometimes been less than enthusiastic about *1984*, which repels them by [what critic Isaac Deutscher calls] its "mystic cruelty" (they generally prefer the more titillating variety found in the novels of [the Marquis] de Sade), while deploring the lack of "progression or surprise in the plot" and the "absence of depth of characterization," comments which indicate that they have failed to grasp that Orwell has written a Menippean satire [a form of satire with a loosely organized narrative and characters who exist only to voice points of view] a genre that tolerates neither of the qualities they claim to be lacking.

But these dissenting and querulously sulky voices are very much in the minority. From its inception the novel was a critical and popular success. Lionel Trilling, doyen of American critics of the time, called the book "profound, terrifying and wholly fascinating." George Steiner called it "a desolate book" but "oblique and highly artful." Edward Thomas went further in referring to it as "a book that towers above . . . almost any novel of our time." Irving Howe, while finding *1984* inferior to Kafka's *The Trial* argues that Orwell's book "is in some ways more terrible." No one who has read *1984* ever forgets it, Howe asserts, "for the book is written out of one passionate breath, each word is bent to a severe discipline of meaning, everything is stripped to the bareness of terror." He continues: "The book appalls us because its terror, far from being inherent in the human condition, is particular to our century; what haunts us is the sickening awareness that in

1984 Orwell has seized upon those elements of public life that, given courage and intelligence, were avoidable."

The Terror of Totalitarianism

The terror referred to here is the terror inherent in totalitarian society, the terror we have seen manifested to its full in [Adolf] Hitler's Germany, [Joseph] Stalin's Russia, Mao [Zedong's] China, and Pol Pot's Kampuchea [Cambodia], to mention only some of the hells of the last 50 years of this bloodstained century. If there is an apocalyptic wildness about *1984* it springs from Orwell's insight into the nature of the murderous politics of the totalitarian state. In Stalin's Russia, 66,000,000 fell victim to this madness; in Hitler's Germany at least 12,000,000; in Mao's China, about 30,000,000; in Pol Pot's Kampuchea, over 2,000,000—and who knows how many elsewhere, in Eastern Europe or Central and South America? The magnitude of this slaughter is mercifully beyond our comprehension, for we cannot grasp the reality of death on this scale.

Confronted with this towering edifice of death, the writer finds himself bereft of his art. To attempt to portray this holocaust in its entirety is beyond the resources of literature. Yet one way to make the tragedy of totalitarianism comprehensible is to reduce the scale of the drama and demonstrate, through the crushing of one man, the extinction of millions. This was Orwell's method in *1984*: to make of Winston Smith and Julia an Everyman and an Everywoman; to shadow forth through their destruction by the state the annihilation of so many anonymous others. To achieve this end, Orwell had to abandon the genres he had used before the war—the realistic novel and the documentary—and turn to fantasy, to the allegory of *Animal Farm*, and the science fiction of *1984*. Since the common sense of the rationalist humanist could no longer comprehend the homicidal psychopathology of contemporary society, Orwell was forced to turn to fantasy to drive his message home. "[British novelist H.G.] Wells is too sane to understand the modern world," Orwell remarked, for he himself believed that civilization had become insane. "The world is suffering from some kind of mental disease which must be diagnosed before it can be cured," he wrote. It was a similar conviction that led Jonathan Swift to write that other great fantasy, *Gulliver's Travels*. But whereas Swift wrote out of an excoriating hatred for mankind—the Yahoo species [vile creatures in *Gulliver's Travels*]—Orwell writes out of a passion for freedom, justice, and, above all, truth. *Gulliver's Travels* was, nevertheless, an important influence on *1984* (as on *Animal Farm*) and there are interesting parallels between Oceania and Books III and IV of Swift's work. For we must never forget that *1984* is above all a Menippean satire in which Orwell reveals that he has learned a great deal of his trade from the savage indignation of that master satirist Swift, whose "terrible intensity of vision, capable of picking out a single hidden truth and then magnifying and distorting it," helps Orwell discern our future lurking in our present. . . .

The Dehumanization of Technology

The dehumanized society of *1984* is . . . a world where the machine has triumphed over man and mechanical over human values. Orwell, a radical in politics but a conservative in all else, had long feared that the machine would come to dominate mankind. As a socialist, he admitted that machines were necessary to rid mankind of drudgery and raise us above the brutes; but he was also afraid that technology would degrade us to a bestial level by making it unnecessary or impossible for us to work. He did not foresee our present crisis in which almost half of the huge and evergrowing army of unemployed throughout both the capitalist and communist worlds owes its enforced idleness directly to automation; but had he lived to see the chaos wrought by such mechanization he would not have been surprised, since he never trusted or liked machine civilization. For Orwell, Nature was essentially good and technology essentially evil. Technology in *1984* is used to enslave men, not liberate them. The telescreen, the speakwrite, the helicopter, the versificators that compose the songs sung by the proles, the book-writing machine on which Julia labors, and all the rest of the technological paraphernalia of the novel exist only to aggrandize the power of the state and violate human nature.

Dr. David A. Goodman, director of the Newport Neuroscience Center in Culver City, California, has found no less than 137 predictions of technological and social change in Orwell's book, from urban police patrol helicopters and helicopter gunships to electronic surveillance and the idea of the leader as an invention of the media. Of these forecasts, over 100 had already been realized by the mid-1970s. Others are like the "speakwrite," a voice-activated typewriter (VAT) which has only just been invented (by IBM's Dr. Frederick Jelenick) and is not yet on the market [in 1984]. Orwell's vision of the future would have been even grimmer had he been aware of the development of the computer, silicon chip technology, mind-altering drugs, and modern weaponry. As it is, the picture he paints of a society in which everyone is under surveillance for 24 hours a day is now not only possible but highly feasible.

The Intelligentsia Has Underrated *1984*

I remarked earlier that *1984* had not been well received by our intelligentsia, who have, for the most part, either undervalued or systematically denigrated this work. The book has met with a great deal of resistance, mainly from the Left, who have objected vociferously and often abusively to Orwell's attack on the Soviet Union, a country which in their eyes is the embodiment of all they revere and therefore can do no wrong. Orwell himself made no apologies for his onslaught on Soviet communism, either in *Animal Farm* or in *1984*. His own harrowing experiences in Spain, combined with his careful observations of Soviet actions both at home and abroad, especially since the rise of Stalin, had convinced him that the Soviet Union was an epicenter of evil that had betrayed its own and every other revolution. In writing *1984* he was deeply influenced by the exiled Russian novelist, Yevgeny Ivanovich Zamyatin (1884–1937), whose satirical work *We*, with its devastating picture of a totalitarian state, was never published in the Soviet Union. . . .

If any book can bear comparison with *1984*, it is [Aleksandr] Solzhenitsyn's masterpiece [*Gulag Archipelago*], whose three volumes constitute an epic of suffering and death which overshadows even Orwell's great book. Yet Solzhenitsyn's work is only one of the accounts of the totalitarian purgatory. A sizable library could surely be assembled from books dealing with totalitarian barbarism in Nazi Germany, the Soviet Union, Mao's China, North Korea, Cuba, Kampuchea or the South American dictatorships. How, then, given this wealth of factual information, much of it compiled at first-hand, is it possible to argue that *1984* is "exaggerated and hysterical," that it springs not from reality but from Orwell's wounded psyche and—as David Daiches puts it—that "it is too obsessed and self-lacerating to arouse serious political reflection"?

The question becomes even more insistent when one realizes that the fall of Hitler and [Benito] Mussolini and the deaths of Stalin and Mao did not by any means spell the end of totalitarianism. Any intellectual who wishes to see what a totalitarian regime is like still has a wide variety to choose from. I remember visiting China in the last years of the Cultural Revolution—an event that resembled Orwell's "Two Minutes' Hate" extended over a decade—and being astonished at how closely China resembled *1984*. . . .

Phrases of Orwell's kept occurring to me as I journeyed through the China of the Gang of Four, especially one that ran: "Anything old, and for that matter anything beautiful, was always vaguely suspect." This could well have been the battle cry of the infamous Red Guards, who systematically destroyed anything old and anything beautiful in the name of ideology. To protest against what was happening was, of course, not only useless but often fatal. As Orwell put it, in words that apply to all totalitarian regimes: "When once you were in the grip of the Party, what you felt or did not feel, what you did or refrained from doing, made literally no difference. Whatever happened you vanished. You were lifted clear out of the stream of history."

In Mao's China some 30,000,000 victims were lifted clear out of the stream of history, generally with a shot in the back of the head, to say nothing of the 50,000,000 or so who perished of hunger in the appalling famines of 1959–1962 that followed the Great Leap Forward—famines for which the Peking government must be held almost wholly responsible. There is as yet no Chinese Solzhenitsyn to describe the workings of a system beside which the Soviet model of terror was clumsy and inefficient. But we have accounts by now of what took place in China under Mao to make us realize the enormity of these events in terms of human tragedy.

How was it, then, that while these events were taking place the Western intellectuals were apparently as unaware of them as they had been blissfully unaware of Stalin's death camps? . . .

Intelligentsia Worship Power, Subvert Democracy

It was precisely this wish to be deceived, this refusal to look at the palatable truth, which Orwell castigated in the intelligentsia of his day. The evidence was there, in front of their eyes, yet they refused to see it. We must not forget that Orwell was, until the end of his days, a convinced socialist who maintained a deep-rooted belief in democracy, which he insisted was the only force capable of resisting the advance of the totalitarian state. "So long as democracy exists," he wrote, "to-

The Warsaw troops' occupation of Prague in 1968 shows the tyranny that comes from failure to resist Marxism, which Orwell warned society of in his novel Nineteen Eighty-Four. © INTERFOTO/History/Alamy.

talitarianism is in deadly danger." Yet, to his dismay, the Left-wing intellectuals, seduced by the specious theories of Marxism, had betrayed democracy and paved the way for totalitarianism by their worship of power and their deliberate distortion of the truth and refusal to face reality. For Orwell, the great disease of the modern world was its worship of power, whether the power of the leader, the power of the state or the power of the machine. Before the triad of power, dehumanized and dehumanizing, the intellectuals of the West had fallen prostrate in worship. As O'Brien says: "The Party seeks power entirely for its own sake. We are not interested in the good of others. . . . We are interested solely in power. Power is inflicting pain and humiliation. Power is in tearing human minds to pieces and putting them together again. . . . If you want a picture of the future, imagine a boot stamping on a human face—forever."

We may object to this explanation of politics as implausible and unsatisfactory. Granted that sadism plays a large part in contemporary politics, it is surely going too far to ascribe all political maneuvering only to sadism. Totalitarian society is ruled by sadism, to be sure; but it is also ruled by greed, envy, hatred, malice, and the rest of the deadly sins. Sadism does not by any means have a monopoly. So the lust for power may be as motivated by pride and greed, for example, as by sadism. Moreover, as Isaac Deutscher has argued, any political party is a social body actuated by interest and purpose, whereas Orwell's party is simply "a phantom-like emanation of all that is foul in human nature . . . the metaphysical, mad and triumphant, Ghost of Evil."

Nevertheless, though Orwell was wrong in envisaging the party only in terms of sadism, he was certainly right in stating that the besetting sin of the intellectuals was to crawl abjectly before power. Since Orwell detested power in any form, whether the power of the state or the power of capital, he could never forgive his fellow intellectuals of the Left for their worship of this false god. "Why do so many socialist intellectuals *want* the state to be all-powerful?" he asked. "Why cannot they understand that many decent people might be repelled by their objectives?"

Orwell came to regard the intelligentsia as essentially underminers of everything "decent," to use his favorite term. "Decency" for Orwell was a comprehensive virtue including truth, liberty, justice, fair play, and compassion. "The thing that frightens me about the modern intelligentsia is their inability to see that human society must be based on common decency," he wrote. For Orwell, intellectuals were, above all, subversive of democracy, an institution he equated with decency. "During the past 25 years, the activities of what are called 'intellectuals' have been almost wholly mischievous. I do not think it an exaggeration to say that if the intellectuals had done their work a little more thoroughly, Britain would have surrendered in 1940."

As George Watson put it: "The intellectual's dream of perfection is for Orwell the nightmare in which men may all soon be slaves." Orwell argued that the intellectuals were often frustrated men of action, romantically fascinated by dictatorship and violence. If this was true of the 1930s, it has proved even more true of our own era where, since the 1960s, many intellectuals have moved steadily to the extreme Left, embracing not only Marxism, but also most forms of extremism and terrorism en route. To quote Watson again: "If Orwell could see them [the intellectuals] now . . . he might still feel he had warned in vain." Or, as Lionel Trilling put it: "No one knows better than he (Orwell) how willing is the intellectual Left to enter the prison of its own mass mind."

Solzhenitsyn has repeatedly and despairingly alleged that the Western democracies have lost the will to resist totalitarianism and are eaten hollow from within by their own moral decay and the termite-like attacks of their radical intellectuals. Here, once again, he finds himself anticipated by Orwell who averred that the ultimate threat to human freedom would not come from the reactionary right, from the champions of class, capital, and privilege, but rather from a Fifth Column, from "the new aristocracy of bureaucrats, scientists, trade-union organizers, publicity experts, sociologists, teachers, journalists, and professional politicians." . . .

Marxism in Universities

Orwell's fears were justified. Since his death only 34 years ago [in 1950], extremism has grown like a cancer to an extent that would have convinced him, had he lived to see it, that the regime he portrayed in *1984* was "slouching towards Bethlehem to be born." The blood-dimmed tide of which [William Butler] Yeats spoke so prophetically has indeed loosed and is spreading like a red stain across the world. It is little wonder that Western universities are permeated through and through with radicalism and Marxism; yet the latter, only 30 years ago, was an alien creed very largely confined to a few hotheads in departments of sociology and economics. Nowadays it is scarcely an exaggeration to say that whole faculties may be deemed Marxist or Marxisant and that in many universities the free play of tolerant debate has given way to an intolerant stifling of controversy in the name of Leftist dogma. If "doublethink" and "duckspeak" are to be found throughout our society today, one must lay the blame where it belongs, at the gates of our institutions of higher learning. What Julien Benda called "*la trahison des clercs*"—"the treason of the intellectuals"—has already occurred, just as Orwell foretold it would. Nor can we afford to dismiss the present ascendancy of Marxism in our universities as simply a harmless piece of eccentricity. From our universities this stultifying doctrine has been systematically exported into every profession and calling that employ graduates, spreading the virus through our schools, our trade unions, our political parties, our bureaucracy, our publishing houses, our media, and even the churches, of whatever denomination. It is this that accounts for the widespread adulation of despotism in the West; for our obdurate refusal to look political reality in the face; for our continual servile willingness to excuse or justify behavior on the part of the totalitarian regimes which would be subject to the strongest expressions of outrage on our part were it to occur elsewhere. . . .

The gist of Orwell's message should by now have become quite clear. Either we resist the onslaught of the Marxists and the machines or civilization perishes. But how strong a resistance can we mount to this troika of totalitarianism, technology, and terror? The answer, I fear, must be a pessimistic one. . . .

1984 Succeeds as a Warning and as Art

Solzhenitsyn has observed that the tragedy of the modern world is that man has forgotten God and so embarked on a moral and spiritual decline that will shortly bring about the collapse of Western civilization and the onset of a long night of cruelty and despotism. He is struck by the irony of the fact that, though democracy has been under sentence of death since the formation of the Comintern in 1919, we do not believe in our own imminent subjugation and refuse to be awakened even though, as he puts it, "the ceiling is falling on our heads." To become aware of our peril, he continues, "the West must hear the voices of those writers, those publicists, those leaders who say: 'We are now already in mortal danger, we are in greater danger than we were in 1940.'"

Orwell is just such a writer, and *1984* was his last attempt to sound the alarm bell and awaken the sleepers before it was too late. Who is to say but that the history of the postwar era might not have been very different without Orwell's warning cry in our ears? "All art is propaganda but not all propaganda is art," said Orwell. *1984* is both effective propaganda and consummate art. As F.R. Learis maintains: "In coming to terms with great literature we discern what at bottom we really believe." Orwell's novel forces us to search our consciences and decide what we ultimately believe in—the uphill path of freedom and responsibility or the downhill path of mindless surrender to state, party, leader, and machine.

In spite of his lack of religious faith and his overreliance on commonsense pragmatism, Orwell was a deeply moral man whose profound commitment to absolute values, especially truth, freedom, and justice, and unflinching courage and resolution brought him very close to the position held by the deeply religious Solzhenitsyn. Like Solzhenitsyn, he has warned us of what our fate will be if we persist in defining ourselves in materialistic and economic terms, forgetting who we really are. "For what shall it profit a man if he gain the whole world and lose his soul?" the Gospel asks us. But as Orwell has chillingly demonstrated, once we lose our souls in this devil's bargain, we lose the whole world as well. This is the lesson we must all soon learn—or perish.

Contemporary Perspectives on the Abuse of Power

Islamic Totalitarianism Is Today's Version of Fascism

Douglas Streusand

Douglas Streusand is an Islamic historian and a professor of military history at the Institute for World Politics, a graduate school of international and security studies.

In the following selection, Streusand argues that, although most Muslims are not active participants in Islamic totalitarianism, many are sympathetic to the movement. Islamic totalitarianism is a threat to the West in the same way that communism was during the Cold War and Nazism during World War II, he asserts. Because of globalization, the fight against Islamic totalitarianism will need to be waged differently than earlier wars. The war will end, Streusand explains, but it will take time.

The al Qaeda operatives who hijacked four airliners [on September 11, 2001], their leaders, and their supporters represented neither Islamic civilization nor the faith of Islam, despite their claims to do so. They served instead a totalitarian ideology known as Islamism, militant Islam, or Islamic totalitarianism. Had the United States treated the attacks as part of a war of civilizations, we would have bolstered the Islamic totalitarian claim to represent and lead the Islamic world, and thus would have strengthened our enemies.

Islamic totalitarianism is a synthesis of the dissident tradition of political activism within Islam and Western totalitarian ideas. The struggle against al Qaeda and the ideology that created it is more a continuation of our parents' and grandparents' wars against fascism and communism than a revival

Douglas Streusand, "The Clash of Civilizations? Islamic Totalitarianism Constitutes an Ideological Threat, as Marxism-Leninism Did During the Cold War," *World and I*, vol. 18, July 2003, p. 20. Copyright © 2003 News World Communications, Inc. Reproduced by permission.

of the Crusades, even though the Islamic totalitarians call their enemies crusaders. [Al Qaeda leader] Osama bin Laden is more a Muslim [Heinrich] Himmler [overseer of the Nazi concentration camps] than a contemporary Saladin [sultan of Egypt and Syria who led Islamic opposition to the Second and Third Crusades]. Islamic totalitarianism has a broad appeal in the Islamic world and constitutes a serious threat, both in the Islamic world and in the West.

Islamic Political Activism

Islamic activism, of which totalitarianism is the contemporary form, is one of three political tempers or attitudes that developed in the early centuries of Islamic history. Because the Prophet Muhammad acted as a political leader and military commander, Islam confronted the problem of political power from its beginning. At Muhammad's death in 632, the Muslim community had to establish new political institutions as well as codify and transmit his religious legacy. Most Muslims accepted the political structures that eventually evolved, most importantly the Abbasid caliphate, as fully legitimate, though the institutions, practices, and symbolic forms of government owed more to pre-Islamic Iran than to Muhammad's rule in Medina.

This pragmatic temper dominated the political order of the Islamic world. Some Muslims believed that no human political institution could reach the moral standard Muhammad had defined and took a quietist stance: avoiding politics, minimizing interaction with the state, and focusing on their personal spiritual concerns. Others, including Sunnis and Shias [two denominations of Islam], believed that the existing political order had become so corrupt that Islam required political action, the destruction of the existing political and social order, and the creation of a new polity to permit Muslims to live in accordance with the aspirations of their faith.

175

In the activist vocabulary, jihad, which literally means "striving" and has a wide variety of connotations, refers to warfare as the mechanism of establishing this just society. The activists maintain that by participating in jihad, Muslims guarantee their own futures in paradise and bring about paradise on earth as well. Failing to do so constitutes shirking a fundamental Muslim duty.

The most important activist theorist, Ibn Taymiyyah (1263–1328), developed this view of jihad and its corollary, takfir. The doctrine of takfir, excommunication, holds that one Muslim may define another as a kafir (infidel), if he fails to undertake the duties of a Muslim, including jihad.

Political activism first emerged, in an inchoate form, in the assassinations of the third and fourth caliphs, 'Uthman and Ali, in 656 and 661. Activist movements have appeared consistently throughout Islamic history; the Nizari Isma'ilis, known in the West as the Assassins, were one.

In some cases, empires were conquered by activists, most notably the Almoravids and Almohads in Spain and North Africa in the eleventh, twelfth, and thirteenth centuries and the Safavis in Iran in the sixteenth century. But when they did so, their governments consistently resembled the regimes that they overthrew. Like other revolutionary movements, premodern and modern, Islamic political activism has consistently devoured its own, and inevitably so. As a utopian ideology it has an agenda it cannot fulfill, for it cannot deliver paradise on earth.

The manifest imperfection of the human condition makes utopian ideologies continually tempting. Karl Popper, among the greatest thinkers of the twentieth century, explains their appeal in *The Open Society and Its Enemies*: "They give expression to a deep-felt dissatisfaction with a world which does not, and cannot, live up to our moral ideals and to our dreams of perfection." Because Islam encompasses politics, some Muslims will always seek perfection through politics. Islamic political activism has been, and will be, a persistent force in the politics of the Islamic world, where, historically, it has been only sporadically successful.

The Encounter with the West

The Islamic world's encounter with the modern West, however, gave an enormous impetus to Islamic political activism and engendered Islamic totalitarianism. The Western totalitarianisms developed out of the political, social, economic, and cultural turbulence produced by the Industrial Revolution. The Islamic world suffered an even greater disruption. Urbanization, industrialization, global communication, and economic integration produced dramatic social and economic disruption. But Western political, military, and economic superiority, which was obvious by the beginning of the nineteenth century, challenged not only the political and economic structures of the Islamic world but the cultural assumptions of most Muslims.

Muslims regarded their worldly political success, marked by continuous territorial expansion, as one of the proofs of the superiority of Islam. In the early modern era, three Muslim empires, the Ottoman, Safavi (Azerbaijan), and Mughal (North India), were among the greatest powers of the world. By 1800, the Safavi empire had disappeared entirely, the Mughals were only figureheads, and the Ottoman empire had become the "sick man" of Europe, surviving only because the European powers could not decide how to partition it.

Many Muslims marveled at the power of the West and sought to explain it. Nasir al-Din Shah Qajar, the ruler of Iran, wrote of the English after he visited Britain in 1874: "One sees and comprehends that they are a great people, and that the Lord of the Universe has bestowed upon them power and might, sense and wisdom, and enlightenment. Thus it is that they have conquered a country like India, and hold important possessions in America and elsewhere in the world."

This statement shows the awe that Western power created in the minds of many Muslims. With that awe came self-doubt and resentment. How could Europeans have achieved such supremacy? How, in the face of it, could Muslims maintain the superiority of their faith?

Jamal al-Din al-Afghani (1838–1897), the founder of modern Islamic political activism and thus the precursor of Islamic totalitarianism, asserted that the abandonment of Islamic practices weakened the Islamic world:

> The times have been so cruel and life so hard and confusing that some Muslims . . . have lost patience and assert . . . that Islamic principles are their oppressors and then give up using religious principles of justice in their actions. They resort, even, to the protection of a foreign power. . . . Actually the schisms and divisions which have occurred in Muslim states originate only from the failure of rulers who deviate from the solid principles upon which the Islamic faith is built and stray from the road followed by their early ancestors. Certainly, opposition to solidly based precepts and wandering away from customary ways are the very actions that are most damaging to power. When those who rule Islam return to the rules of their law and model their conduct upon that practiced by early Muslims, it will not be long before God gives them extensive power and bestows strength upon them comparable to that wielded by the orthodox caliphs, who were leaders of the faith.

This passage, written in 1884, sounds strikingly contemporary. Al-Afghani's call for a return to the "solidly based precepts and customary ways" of the early Islamic empires did not represent a conservative impulse, though he presented it as such, but a radical one. By implication al-Afghani condemned all the Muslim governments of his time for compromising with the West and attempting to develop modern institutions to compete with Western powers. Though ultimately directed against the West, his program required a radical alter-

A mural in Tehran's Enghelab Square depicting Iran's supreme leader, Ayatollah Ali Khamenei, conveys a "down with America" sentiment. Historian Douglas Streusand draws a correlation between Islamic totalitarianism's threat to the West and the Nazi threat during World War II. Behrouz Mehri/AFP/Getty Images.

ation of Muslim institutions and polities. In the twentieth century, this program for radical change became Islamic totalitarianism.

Islamic Totalitarian Doctrines

Three major thinkers brought about this transformation: Sayyid Abu al-'Ala' Mawdudi (1903–1979) of Pakistan, Sayyid Qutb (1906–1966) of Egypt, and Ruhollah Khomeini (1902–1989) of Iran. A brief examination of their views reveals how they combined Islamic activism with modern Western ideas, most importantly [Vladimir] Lenin's concept of the party as the vanguard of the proletariat.

Lenin conceived of a political party that would lead the working class into revolution, creating a revolutionary consciousness. Mawdudi seized upon this idea and established the Jama'at-I Islami in Pakistan to serve as such a party. Mawdudi sought not proletarian revolution but the establishment of an

Islamic state. Qutb and Khomeini borrowed this concept from Mawdudi; Khomeini established the Islamic Republic Party in Iran for this purpose.

The biographies of these three ideologues also show that they had a foot in each world. Only Khomeini had a traditional Islamic religious education; the title of ayatollah by which he is generally known indicates that he reached the highest rank of the hierarchy of Shia ulama (community of learned men). For all his traditional appearance, Khomeini was not a traditional thinker. He drew on the works of Mawdudi and Qutb as well as traditional Shia texts.

The Iranian author and journalist Amir Taheri asserts that Khomeini learned to hate the Jews from Nazi propaganda broadcasts in Arabic. Khomeini's doctrine of the "government of the jurist," though presented in traditional terms, broke ground in several ways. Although the Shia ulama had been increasingly assertive in politics since the late seventeenth century, none had claimed the right to govern for themselves. In the 1920s, the ulama of Iran had demanded that Reza Khan take the throne as Reza Shah rather than establish a republic. A generation later, Khomeini maintained that the ulama, led by a supreme religious leader, should actually govern in its own name. None of the other leading ayatollahs accepted this doctrine; the late Elie Kedourie labeled it "political heresy."

Both Qutb and Mawdudi had modern secular educations and knew the West well. Qutb spent 1948–51 in the United States. His experience appalled him. He described the United States as a country full of churches but without religion, stained with sexual immorality, tainted by racism, materially successful but morally hollow. Qutb believed the West was so overwhelmingly materialistic that a communist triumph was inevitable.

He interpreted the Prophet Muhammad as a revolutionary whose triumph ended the jahiliyah, the era of ignorance, of tribal polytheism, in Arabia. He conceived of the modern world as a new jahiliyah, "grounded in knowledge, complexity, and scorn." Western knowledge constitutes, for Qutb, ignorance because it leads the minds of humanity away from God and divine law. He calls upon Muslims to imitate Muhammad and destroy the new jahiliyah, as he did the old one.

Many Muslims Sympathize with Islamic Totalitarianism

Despite its revolutionary character and the harsh repression it brings, Islamic totalitarianism has a broad appeal in the Islamic world. Estimates of the proportion of Muslims who support it vary enormously, from a tiny minority to a substantial moiety. In all probability, the percentage of actual, active participants in the totalitarian movement is small, though a small percentage of the world's billion Muslims is still a large number. A much larger proportion, however, does not accept the totalitarian ideology or want to live under a government like that of the Taliban but nonetheless sympathizes with the totalitarians to a degree.

Muslims have the best of reasons for wanting change. Many live in poverty under repressive authoritarian regimes. Rapid economic and social changes have produced widespread alienation and uncertainty. Muslims naturally want the freedom, power, and prosperity they see in the West but distrust Western ideas and institutions. Islamic totalitarianism promises a way out, with empowerment and social justice on earth as well as eternity in paradise. The hope is false but enormously attractive to populations who trust no other alternative. Islamic totalitarians portray their ideology as the only alternative to the West, and Muslims want an alternative. Many of them perceive the West as Sayyid Qutb did: materialistic, immoral, wanton, violent. The West's portrayal of itself in movies, television, music videos, and video games supports that perception.

Many Muslims, seeing their recent history as a record of defeat and despair, yearn for victories to restore their pride. The September 11 attacks appeared to them as a great victory over an arrogant opponent that other Arab and Muslim powers had failed to humble. The swift victory over the Taliban in Afghanistan and now the destruction of the Baath regime in Iraq, without any effective response from al Qaeda, have significantly weakened the standing of that group but not eliminated the totalitarian temptation.

Confronting Islamic Totalitarianism

Islamic totalitarianism, then, constitutes an ideological threat, as Marxism-Leninism did during the Cold War. As Eliot Cohen, James Woolsey, and others have suggested, the struggle against it constitutes a world war, as the Cold War did, and will resemble the Cold War in nature and duration. Victory will require military preparation, military action, and a whole range of nonmilitary actions over a long term, perhaps more than a generation.

Marxism-Leninism and Nazism were deadly threats to the West not only because of their ideological appeal but because they controlled major industrial powers. Islamic totalitarianism has no such base. The enormous changes of the past several decades, which we refer to as globalization, have made the entire world extremely vulnerable to asymmetric warfare, with or without weapons of mass destruction. Deterrence, the idiom of the Cold War, cannot work against the Islamic totalitarians because they lack assets for us to hold hostage to our retaliation. The destruction of al Qaeda will not end the struggle, because Islamic totalitarianism does not depend on a single head or center. The elimination of every single al Qaeda operative would be an enormous victory but would not end the war.

The war will end as, gradually, the hollowness of Islamic totalitarianism becomes clear and it loses its mass appeal. As it

did in the premodern era, pragmatism will triumph over activism. That process will take several dangerous decades.

Autocracies Are Threatened by the Financial Crisis

Joshua Kurlantzick

Joshua Kurlantzick is a senior correspondent at the American Prospect *and a special correspondent at the* New Republic.

In the following viewpoint, Kurlantzick asserts that the existing global economic crisis creates a tenuous situation for the autocratic nations of the world—those in which all the political power is concentrated in the hands of one person. Modern dictatorships have maintained power over their citizens by promising them prosperity—trading financial security for individual liberties. The downturn in the global economy, Kurlantzick states, is being felt in Venezuela, Russia, China, and Persian Gulf states, and social unrest has broken out in these areas as a result.

Gansu is one of interior China's most forlorn provinces, one that has gone largely unnoticed by the outside world. When I worked in rural Gansu two years ago [in 2007], I met few people who had ever left their hometown. In one tiny village, ethnic minority Muslims were eking out a living as farmers in the dusty, arid climate and sleeping in simple stone huts that looked like they'd been built centuries earlier. Most villagers had never met a foreigner before.

Then last fall, Gansu suddenly hit the news. Some 2,000 people rioted in one district, torching cars, smashing up the local Communist Party offices, and attacking policemen with iron rods, chains, and axes in protest of a local government decision that might have forced some of them to resettle.

Gansu isn't the only Chinese province that has erupted in social unrest lately. Taxi drivers have gone on strike in several

Joshua Kurlantzick, "Twilight of the Autocrats: Will the Financial Crisis Bring Down Russia and China?" *The American Prospect*, vol. 20, March 2009, pp. 32–34.

Chinese cities, people who lost money in illegal fundraising have protested in Beijing, and demonstrators have gathered across the country to demand unpaid back wages. Protest has even spread to the Pearl River Delta, the manufacturing center that abuts Hong Kong, traditionally one of the most prosperous parts of the country. In some years, the Delta's factories have produced 5 percent of all manufactured goods made in the world. But orders for the Delta's products have dried up, and angry factory workers, many owed back pay, have taken to looting warehouses. As these protests turn violent, they could provoke a violent response; Chinese factory owners are increasingly hiring thugs to hit back at demonstrators.

Economic Downturn Threatens Dictatorships

The protests hint at something even bigger than China: The economic downturn has created a profound threat to the autocratic regimes of the world, from China and Russia to Venezuela and the Persian Gulf states. Already, the Russian police have been placed on alert to crack down on demonstrators. Several of Russia's prominent human-rights activists have been killed in recent weeks. Protests, once rare, have spread from eastern Russia to the heart of the Kremlin itself.

Modern autocracies are very different from those of the past. Rather than ruling by strict ideology, ruthless internal police, and tight control of information, authoritarian regimes like Beijing and Moscow have remained in power primarily by making an implicit bargain with their most critical middle-class citizens—you might not have freedom, but you will have money. As long as the broad middle class, which is where the most dangerous dissent would take hold, is gaining ground economically, the regime is safe.

So while in the West, leaders worry that the global economy faces a second Great Depression, such an economic crisis poses a major threat to some of the world's most resilient autocracies. A strong economy was their only backstop. Now, starved of the growth that keeps them in power and unable to repress their people as old-fashioned dictators did, these autocracies may have nothing left to fall back on.

Economic Success Kept Autocracies Stable

Over the past decade, authoritarian capitalist countries built impressive economic resumés. China has grown by over 10 percent in most years, and some of its biggest cities, like Shanghai, now boast per-capita incomes of more than $7,000 per year, the same level as a middle-income nation. Russia, all but bankrupt in the late 1990s, has delivered strong enough growth that it now boasts the third-largest capital reserves in the world and has built its gas companies into such powerhouses that they now dominate the markets of Europe. The authoritarian capitalists proved so successful, in fact, that some in the West began wondering whether their model of development had surpassed liberal democratic capitalism. Israeli political theorist Azar Gat argued in *Foreign Affairs* [in 2008] that the most significant challenge to liberal democracy today "emanates from the rise of non-democratic great powers: the West's old Cold War rivals China and Russia, now operating under authoritarian capitalist, rather than communist, regimes."

Constant growth kept the populations quiet. In Russia, [then-president] Vladimir Putin promised to save the country from the ruin of the 1990s, a time when Russians enjoyed a more open society but incomes and wages fell sharply. True democracy, he implicitly suggested, might result in disorder in such a large and unwieldy nation. And in return for higher growth rates and greater disposable income, Russians allowed Putin to slowly strangle their freedoms. "Putin does provide stability of sorts, which the middle classes cherish," says Dmitri Trenin of the Carnegie Endowment's Moscow Center. "Even those [Russians] who oppose authoritarianism in principle fear that the likely alternatives are worse—outright chaos, populist nationalism, much harsher authoritarianism than Putin's."

In China, the regime made a similar bargain, if not with the masses, at least with its urban middle classes. The regime's investment and largesse was slanted toward the big cities. As Deng Xiaoping vowed when he opened Chinas economy, "Some will get rich first"—and those *nouveau riche* would appreciate who paid for their cars, homes, and glittery new mobile phones. In recent years, according to China expert Jonathan Unger, the government has made a deliberate policy of favoring this population.

In a poll by the Pew Research Center, over 80 percent of Chinese said they were satisfied with conditions in their country, among the highest of responses in the world. Even after two terms in office, Vladimir Putin enjoyed popularity ratings that would be the envy of any Western leader. When I traveled across urban, eastern China two years ago asking young Chinese their view of the government, I found what seemed like a striking amount of political inertia among young elites. "We don't have any control over these things," one middle-class young woman told me in Shanghai, before asking if I'd seen the latest episodes of *The Wire* on DVD.

Autocratic Economies Depend on Exports

The true test of any government, though, comes not in good times but in bad. The autocracies are particularly poorly prepared for a global economic crisis because they have weak domestic consumer markets and rely upon exports to survive. Powerful authoritarian regimes like Russia and the Persian Gulf states are dependent on exports of petroleum or one sole commodity. In Venezuela, energy accounts for some 95 percent of all export revenue. In Iran, it provides some 80 percent of revenues. But the price of oil has dropped by more than half in the past six months. And China, which depends

Job seekers gather outside a job fair in Zhengzhou, China. The worldwide economic crisis that began in 2008 has made it difficult for college graduates to find employment. Bai Zhoufeng/ChinaFotoPress/Getty Images.

largely on exporting manufactured goods to wealthy nations, will also suffer from the financial crisis as consumer spending drops in the U.S., Europe, and Japan. Exports constitute nearly 35 percent of China's gross domestic product [GDP]—far too high a figure to be considered a balanced economy. (U.S. exports account for about 10 percent of GDP most years.)

Despite valiant efforts to assure their people that nothing is wrong, the autocrats cannot cover their economic holes. In Venezuela, [President] Hugo Chavez, after first mocking the financial crisis as a danger to the West, now admits, "The fall in oil prices due to the current global financial crisis may have a negative influence on the economy of Venezuela." In Russia, where the stock market has fallen by some 70 percent since [spring 2008] and the ruble has weathered fierce attacks, Vladimir Putin recently declared he would launch new tax cuts because of the steep drop in Russia's economy. As Stephen Sestanovich of the Council on Foreign Relations notes, "Russia is confronting virtually all the negatives at once—sharply declining export earnings from energy and metals, overleveraged corporate balance sheets and a chorus of bailout appeals, a credit crunch and banking failures, a bursting real-estate bubble."

Challenges to Governments Occurring

While unemployment, poverty, and unrest indicate cracks in the system of autocracy, there are signs that a nascent movement toward liberal democracy could take its place. Indeed, increasing numbers of Chinese are challenging the government, and in December [2008], 303 Chinese intellectuals signed and published a daring manifesto called Charter 08, which demands an end to one-party rule.

Charter 08 is only one sign that the autocracies are feeling the pressure. In Venezuela, Chavez's allies lost ground to opposition parties in recent regional elections. In Russia, a worried President Dmitri Medvedev recently instructed police to stamp out social unrest caused by the downturn. In December [2008], the police arrested some 100 people at a protest in the poor eastern city of Vladivostok; at roughly the same time, 1,000 people attended a protest in Moscow against the government. Even in the Persian Gulf and Central Asian states, normally some of the quietest parts of the world, the crisis has had political consequences. Kazakh activists have started holding rallies against the government, previously a rare occurrence in the country. Iran, too, faces instability. Inflation in the Islamic Republic is now running near 30 percent, and a powerful cleric mused publicly that the crisis could do "big damage."

The autocrats clearly are worried. In addition to cracking down on the Charter 08 signers and other activists, Beijing recently announced a stimulus package worth $586 billion. In Gansu, local officials actually met with the protest leaders and vowed to invest some $3 billion in the area.

The autocracies have money to burn. China has stockpiled nearly $2 trillion but is eating it up fast. Russia is spending nearly $10 billion a week defending the ruble, to little avail, as the value of the currency keeps plummeting. Though they can plow money into their economies, the autocratic leaders cannot make Western consumers shop or guzzle gas and so are powerless to control their major economic engines. And if regimes like Chavez's try to get their economies under control by cutting government spending, they risk undermining their own power, which was bolstered by government social-welfare programs that often targeted the middle classes whose support they now need.

Crisis Could Doom Autocracies

Unlike 20th-century autocrats such as Fidel Castro, who led their countries in wars of independence, most of today's leaders came up through the political system and have no revolutionary bona fides to play. The modern authoritarian governments long ago abandoned real ideology. (Chavez is an exception: He has tried to fashion a modern statist ideology he calls the "Bolivarian Revolution.") China remains a nominally communist country, but if Karl Marx were to visit today, he would be horrified. With policies that favor the urban elite and virtually no social welfare programs left, this "communist" nation has become one of the most unequal societies in Asia.

Lacking any ideology other than sour nationalism, the new autocrats cannot rally their population in down times by appealing to their political idealism, as they did in the 1950s and early 1960s, when ideology kept the government in control during massive famines. And while these nations have sophisticated security apparatuses, their leaders have allowed enough freedom for the economy to grow—which means it's too late to brainwash their citizens or to create a personality cult like Kim Jong-Il's in North Korea. Despite Putin's crackdown on the Russian press, liberal-opposition media outlets are still in business, and average Russians can access most Internet sites.

In order to improve their standing on the world stage, today's autocrats at least try to create the facade of democracy. Their people know about democratic movements in other countries, can access free media, and are not easily subdued. Because the authoritarian governments have created some semblance of a legal system, workers have begun to think they have rights. Compared to the 1980s, when word of demonstrations in China was passed from person to person, today middle-class demonstrators organize by text message, and news of protests quickly appears on Chinese blogs. Chinese and foreign reporters can also follow protests, making it harder for the security forces to get away with a real crackdown.

Neither the short term nor the long term looks good for Moscow, Beijing, and the other autocrats. In the near future, their economies will slow down severely and, in the case of Russia, likely fall into a serious recession. In China, many analysts believe unemployment will rise to its highest level in a decade. Growth is likely to dip below 8 percent, the magic number needed to keep creating enough jobs for all the people entering the work force in China.

Millions of Chinese migrant workers who can no longer find factory jobs will return to the interior of the country. Back in rural areas, anger is already rising. These unemployed workers, who have seen the wealth of urban elites in cities like Shanghai, could begin organizing larger demonstrations, smashing up local Communist Party offices and even attacking local officials. Middle-class protests are likely to rise as well—over issues of government competence like safety, land prices, and land evictions. Since the urbanites have media connections, they are able to get their stories onto Chinese blogs and news sites. Recently, parents of Chinese children who were made ill or died from tainted milk gathered together to push the government for better health care, refusing the regime's attempts to essentially buy them off: (The government recently sentenced two people to death for playing a key role in the tainted-milk scandal.)

Thus far, the autocracies have kept groups of people with grievances against the government from forming united fronts. Moscow has achieved this through the skillful use of nationalism, which drives a wedge between liberal Russians and ethnic minorities with grievances against the government. Beijing has used a combination of crackdowns and payoffs to top demonstrators to keep labor protests separate from one another, preventing them from developing a common theme or common leaders.

Divide and conquer, though, won't work forever. In China, rural and urban protests might soon begin to link up—through activist networks, religious groups, or blogs—and form a national protest. Charter 08 and a nationwide taxi-driver strike, both organized on the Internet, are a first hint of this nationwide movement.

The Great Depression fed dangerous new autocratic ideologies like fascism and communism; a second Great Depression could destroy them. While the economic crisis will cause untold human suffering in these and other countries, it is quite possible that, on the other side of it, we will see the end of that distinctive phenomenon of the late 1990s and early 21st century: the growth autocracy. And that, at least, would bring some light to a financial dark age.

Wiretapping by the George W. Bush Administration Was Illegal and Should Be Investigated

Patrick Radden Keefe

Patrick Radden Keefe, a fellow at the Century Foundation, is the author of Chatter: Uncovering the Echelon Surveillance Network and the Secret World of Global Eavesdropping.

Keefe asserts in the following viewpoint that the George W. Bush administration illegally eavesdropped on the phone conversations of its citizens following the terrorist attacks of September 11, 2001. The program has been stopped, but the question of immunity from prosecution remains. While President Barack Obama has said he does not want to engage in a "partisan witch hunt," he has committed to have the attorney general conduct a review of National Security Agency surveillance. Beyond this, Keefe argues, Congress should conduct hearings on the wiretapping activities. Without some understanding of what went wrong, it is difficult to prevent its happening again in the future, he maintains.

If you thought the wiretapping controversy ended last summer [2008], when Congress blessed the [George W.] Bush administration's warrantless-wiretapping program by passing a new surveillance law that greatly enhanced the powers of the National Security Agency [N.S.A.], think again. The legacy of the illegal operation represents a serious problem for the [Barack] Obama administration.

Wiretapping Questions Remain

After a contentious hearing this month [December 2008] on the most controversial aspect of the new law—a blanket grant of immunity to the telecom giants like AT&T that secretly permitted the N.S.A. to siphon off their customers' communications—a federal judge in San Francisco must decide whether Congress has the authority to bestow absolution on private companies that appear to have violated the law. One paradox is that Bush administration lawyers have claimed from the outset that the surveillance program was entirely legal, yet they remain desperate to prevent any court from testing that claim. Instead, they are in the odd position of advocating immunity for something that they insist is not a crime.

Another paradox, which Barack Obama surely appreciates, is that the real issue underlying the immunity debate is not whether the telecoms should pay damages; it is whether lawsuits against the companies can be used to answer a question that Congress and the press have not: Just how bad was the N.S.A. program, after all?

Mr. Obama says he does not want his first term to become bogged down in any sort of "partisan witch hunt." Indeed, the sheer extent of executive lawlessness in Washington over the past eight years [of the Bush administration] has left so many wrongs to right that, in the interests of triage, the new president may choose to let bygones be bygones where wiretapping is concerned.

But that would be a mistake. From 2001 to 2007, the United States government violated one of the signature prohibitions of the post-Watergate era by turning its formidable eavesdropping apparatus on its own citizens. The new law last summer resolved matters only by moving the goalpost, so that many of the N.S.A.'s more questionable activities simply became legal. But major questions remain about the legal grounds used to justify the program, and about how many innocent Americans were ensnared.

Congress Should Conduct Public Hearings

The Obama administration cannot enact the kind of thorough course correction on domestic surveillance that is needed without understanding how far off course the intelligence community got in the first place. Mr. Obama, who initially vowed to filibuster the immunity provision but, under pressure in the race against John McCain, backed down and reluctantly supported it, has committed "to have my attorney general conduct a comprehensive review" of N.S.A. surveillance.

That is a promising first step, but it is not enough. Nor is the prospect of reports due next summer [2009] from the inspectors general of the N.S.A. and the Justice Department. The good news for Mr. Obama, politically, is that the executive branch should not lead the charge in investigating the wiretapping. Congress should.

Provided that the Obama administration is willing to cooperate rather than stonewall in the Bush fashion, Congress can get to the bottom of the abuses while simultaneously reasserting itself as a coequal branch of government. To the extent possible, the hearings should be public, and if necessary, investigators should grant immunity to witnesses in exchange for candid testimony; this is no witch hunt, but an effort to establish an accurate historical record.

What details can actually be aired in public without violating national security? The number of Americans listened to and the broad contours of the program, for a start. For example, in March 2004, Attorney General John Ashcroft threatened to resign over the program, backing down only when it was adjusted. What transgression was so appalling that it made John Ashcroft look like a civil libertarian? We still don't know.

Even the legal opinions governing the program are still squirreled away in a safe in Vice President Dick Cheney's office. In recent months, the Senate Judiciary Committee and a

Washington district judge have ordered them turned over, and the next attorney general should do so immediately.

Without some baseline understanding of what went wrong—and how wrong—in recent years, and without the establishment of some bright line rules of the road, it would be naïve to think that there won't be future abuses. For aggressive intelligence agencies, legal ambiguity is an invitation to excess.

Wiretapping can sometimes seem forbiddingly complex, and many Americans just aren't concerned that the government might monitor their calls. But what is at stake here is not mere personal privacy, but the bedrock American principles of separation of powers and the rule of law.

Jack Goldsmith, a former top Bush administration lawyer, pronounced the wiretapping program "the biggest legal mess" he had seen in his life. That sort of mess cannot simply be swept under the rug; it must be cleared up.

Technology Makes Surveillance More Prevalent

Peter Funt

Peter Funt is the son of Allen Funt, the creator of the television show Candid Camera. *He is a writer and TV host.*

In the following viewpoint, Funt explains that Street View, a recent technology development by Google, has been termed "Orwellian" because it allows anyone the ability to observe the activities of ordinary citizens. Funt, whose father was famous for catching people on camera in embarrassing moments, sides with those who consider Google's new service an invasion of privacy.

"There was of course no way of knowing whether you were being watched at any given moment ... It was even conceivable that they watched everybody all the time."

That quote from George Orwell's *1984* becomes increasingly prescient in light of developments in eavesdropping, pioneered by Google. Recently the company launched a service called Latitude, which allows consenting users to monitor each other's whereabouts. It's the company's latest snooping tool, the most controversial being the Street Views photographic mapping service.

When I tried Street Views by entering my address, I was surprised to see that with a single click a truly Orwellian image popped onto the screen: my house, my car, the newspaper in the driveway. I could zoom in for a clear view of the open window on the second floor and the handy drain pipe that potential burglars might use to reach that window when no one was home.

Peter Funt, "Google Is Watching," *The Boston Globe*, February 9, 2009, p. A13. Reproduced by permission of the author.

Google's Street View hires motorists to capture panoramic images along many streets. Peter Funt notes that observing citizens this way is reminiscent of the constant surveillance Orwell depicts in Nineteen Eighty-Four. *© amc/Alamy.*

Google has been working on Street Views for nearly two years, an incredibly tedious process. As remarkable as the computer results are, they still require hired motorists, known as Geoimmersive Data Producers, to drive up and down every street using 11 roof-mounted cameras to snap 360-degree images.

Boston was among the first cities captured by Street Views, but much of Massachusetts remains unphotographed. For example, a two-hour drive from a friend's house in Lenox to my daughter's college in Norton yields only two photos: the entrance to the Mass. Pike and, 96 miles later, the exit to I-495.

But when Street Views does come to a community, it tends to spark great curiosity and raging debate about the propriety of Google's remarkable feat. To some, it is an outrageous invasion of privacy—a true step toward the world Orwell envisioned. To others, including Google management, it is simply the latest beneficial—and commercially valuable—use of modern technology.

After arguing that Street Views showed nothing more than could be seen by anyone traveling on public property, Google agreed to blur all identifiable faces and license plates. But by conceding that much, Google opens the door to demands that, say, doors should be blurred, and for that matter upstairs windows and drain pipes.

Of course, it would be naive to think that Big Brother hasn't been watching for some time. From the all-too-obvious ceiling cameras in convenience stores to the government's exotic keyhole satellites, we're all photographed more often than we might care to believe.

[In January 2009] when US Airways Flight 1549 went down unexpectedly in the Hudson River—not a likely spot for routine surveillance—hidden cameras on shore were able to capture it from several angles.

The federal government has already warned Google not to photograph military installations. Then there's North Oaks, Minn., whose city council contacted Google on behalf of its 4,500 residents, demanding that all photos taken within its borders be deleted.

Existing law makes distinctions between public property and private property; between public figures and private individuals. Yet in the Google Universe, these boundaries become fuzzy.

What if I created a reality show for which I stationed a TV crew on the public street outside your house, and spent weeks photographing your every move? What if I edited the footage to make the funniest three minutes—including the time you backed the car over the tulips, and the time you chased the neighbor's cat and slipped? And what if, unlike *Candid Camera*, the show my father Allen Funt invented in 1948, I televised it without your permission?

Or, what if I paid a team of Data Producers to go through thousands of Street Views, including the one with your home, looking for driveways in need of repair, then sold the list to a paving company?

With each technological breakthrough, some laws will require reexamination. So will our definition of privacy.

As someone who, like my father, devoted many years to photographing unsuspecting people, I can report that the latest developments give me pause. It's one thing to have a brief, once-in-a-lifetime encounter with a hidden camera. It's another thing to live, as Orwell put it, "in the assumption that every sound you made was overheard, and, except in darkness, every movement scrutinized."

For Further Discussion

1. In Chapter 1 George Orwell, an avowed socialist, writes about his feelings of patriotism during World War II. He states that being patriotic has nothing to do with conservatism and that there is no contradiction between being patriotic and being a socialist. In recent years, politicians have had their patriotism challenged for a variety of reasons. Do you see any parallels with Orwell's position? Explain.

2. In Chapter 1 Christopher Hitchens finds that the verisimilitude of *Nineteen Eighty-Four* is enhanced by Orwell's personal experiences with brutality—first in an English boarding school, then as a police officer in Burma, and later during the Spanish Civil War. Do you see any reflections of these experiences in *Nineteen Eighty-Four*? Describe.

3. In Chapter 2 both John David Frodsham and Stephen Ingle contend that in *Nineteen Eighty-Four* Orwell is warning of the danger that members of the left-wing intelligentsia in the Socialist Party could create a totalitarian society in their lust for power. This prediction did not turn out to be accurate. What in Orwell's background could have caused him to fear this?

4. In Chapter 3 Patrick Radden Keefe believes that the monitoring of international telephone calls by the National Security Agency under the George W. Bush administration was illegal. Do you agree? Support your answer.

For Further Reading

Margaret Atwood, *The Handmaid's Tale*. Toronto: McClelland and Stewart, 1985.

Margaret Atwood, *Oryx and Crake*. New York: Nan A. Talese, 2003.

Ray Bradbury, *Fahrenheit 451*. New York: Ballantine, 1953.

Anthony Burgess, *A Clockwork Orange*. London: Heinemann, 1962.

Cory Doctorow, *Little Brother*. New York: Tom Doherty, 2008.

William Golding, *Lord of the Flies*. London: Faber, 1954.

Aldous Huxley, *Brave New World*. New York: Doubleday, 1932.

Lois Lowry, *The Giver*. Boston: Houghton Mifflin, 1993.

George Orwell, *Animal Farm*. London: Secker & Warburg, 1945.

George Orwell, *Down and Out in Paris and London*. New York: Harper, 1933.

Kurt Vonnegut Jr., *Slaughterhouse-Five; or, the Children's Crusade: A Duty Dance with Death*. New York: Seymour Lawrence/Delacorte, 1969.

Scott Westerfeld, *Uglies*. New York: Simon Pulse, 2005.

Yevgeny Zamyatin, *We*. New York: Dutton, 1924.

Bibliography

Books

Keith Alldritt — *The Making of George Orwell: An Essay in Literary History.* New York: St. Martin's Press, 1969.

Hannah Arendt — *The Origins of Totalitarianism.* New York: Harcourt, Brace, 1951.

John Atkins — *George Orwell: A Literary Study.* London: J. Calder, 1954.

Anthony Burgess — *1985.* Boston: Little, Brown, 1978.

Jenni Calder — *Huxley and Orwell, "Brave New World" and "Nineteen Eighty-Four."* London: Edward Arnold, 1976.

David Ciepley — *Liberalism in the Shadow of Totalitarianism.* Cambridge, MA: Harvard University Press, 2006.

Ross Clark — *The Road to Big Brother: One Man's Struggle Against the Surveillance Society.* New York: Encounter Books, 2009.

Mark Connelly — *The Diminished Self: Orwell and the Loss of Freedom.* Pittsburgh: Dusquesne University Press, 1987.

Audrey Coppard and Bernard Crick — *Orwell Remembered.* London: British Broadcasting Corp., 1984.

Peter Davison   *George Orwell: A Literary Life.* New York: St. Martin's Press, 1996.

Miriam Gross, ed.   *The World of George Orwell.* London: Weidenfeld and Nicolson, 1971.

Michael Halberstam   *Totalitarianism and the Modern Conception of Politics.* New Haven, CT: Yale University Press, 1999.

Irving Howe, ed.   *Orwell's "Nineteen Eighty-Four": Text, Sources, Criticism.* New York: Harcourt Brace, & World, 1963.

Samuel Hynes, ed.   *Twentieth-Century Interpretations of "1984": A Collection of Critical Essays.* Englewood Cliffs, NJ: Prentice-Hall, 1971.

Ejner J. Jensen, ed.   *The Future of "Nineteen Eighty-Four."* Ann Arbor: University of Michigan Press, 1984.

Valerie Meyers   *George Orwell.* New York: St. Martin's Press, 1991.

Michael Shelden   *Orwell: The Authorized Biography.* New York: HarperCollins, 1991.

Aleksandras Shtromas   *Totalitarianism and the Prospects for World Order: Closing the Door on the Twentieth Century.* Lanham, MD: Lexington Books, 2003.

Peter Stansky and William Abrahams   *The Unknown Orwell.* New York: Knopf, 1972.

Richard J.   *The Paradox of George Orwell.* West
Voorhees   Lafayette, IN: Purdue University
                     Press, 1986.

George Woodcock *The Crystal Spirit: A Study of George
                     Orwell.* Boston: Little, Brown, 1966.

Periodicals

Peter Beinart   "The Good Fight," *New Republic,*
                     December 20, 2004.

Jay Bergman   "Reading Fiction to Understand the
                     Soviet Union: Soviet Dissidents on
                     Orwell's *1984*," *History of European
                     Ideas,* vol. 23, nos. 5–6, 1997.

Robert Christgau   "Writing for the People," *Village
                     Voice,* February 1, 1983.

College Literature   vol. 11, no. 1, 1984. (Issue devoted to
                     studies of *Nineteen Eighty-Four.*)

R. Bruce Douglass "The Fate of Orwell's Warning,"
                     *Thought: A Review of Culture and
                     Idea,* September 1985.

Newt Gingrich   "The Evil Empire," *American
                     Heritage,* Spring-Summer 2008.

Jonah Goldberg   "All About 'Fascism,'" *National
                     Review,* September 25, 2006.

David Goodman   "Orwell's *1984*: The Future Is Here,"
                     Insight on the News, December 31,
                     2001.

Harold J. Harris	"Orwell's Essays and *1984*," *Twentieth-Century Literature*, January 1959.
Michael Isikoff and Evan Thomas	"The Lawyer and the Caterpillar," *Newsweek*, April 27, 2009.
Anthony Kearney	"Orwell's *Animal Farm* and *1984*," *Explicator*, Summer 1996.
Christopher Lasch	"*1984*: Are We There?" *Salmagundi*, Fall 1984.
Leo Mates	"Ring Out Orwell's *1984*," *Contemporary Review*, August 1985.
Modern Fiction Studies	Spring 1975. (Issue devoted to Orwell criticism.)
John Newsinger	"*Nineteen Eighty-Four* Since the Collapse of Communism," *Foundation: The Review of Science Fiction*, Autumn 1992.
Philip Rahv	"The Unfuture of Utopia," *Partisan Review*, July 1949.
Robert Paul Resch	"Utopia, Dystopia, and the Middle Class in George Orwell's *Nineteen Eighty-Four*," *Boundary 2: An International Journal of Literature and Culture*, Spring 1997.
Philip Rieff	"George Orwell and the Post-Liberal Imagination," *Kenyon Review*, Winter 1954.

Mark Ray
Schmidt

"Rebellion, Freedom, and Other Philosophical Issues in Orwell's *1984*," *Publications of the Arkansas Philological Association*, Spring 1996.

Marcus Smith

"The Wall of Blackness: A Psychological Approach to *1984*," *Modern Fiction Studies*, Winter 1968–1969.

Tzvetan Todorov

"Politics, Morality, and the Writer's Life: Notes on George Orwell," *Stanford French Review*, vol. 16, no. 1, 1992.

Index